To my outdoorsy
brother-in-law —
Merry Christmas.
Hope you enjoy!
Love
Burr

MIRROR OF AMERICA

MIRROR OF
Literary Encounters with

John Muir
Ralph Waldo
Emerson — Henry
James — Owen Wister
Abraham Lincoln — Mary
Roberts Rinehart · Rudyard
Kipling — John Burroughs —
Harriet Monroe · Carl Sandburg
Thomas Wolfe · George Catlin
— Frederick Law Olmsted —
James Bryce · Charles
Dickens · Bayard Taylor
Mark Twain · Wallace
Stegner · Bernard
De Voto

NATIONAL PARK FOUNDATION
WASHINGTON

AMERICA
the National Parks

ROBERTS RINEHART, INC. PUBLISHERS
BOULDER

The publisher gratefully acknowledges the permission granted by the following copyright owners to reprint material contained in this volume: *Harper's Magazine* for Owen Wister's "Old Yellowstone Days"; the literary estate of Mary Roberts Rinehart for "Ride the Rockies and Save Your Soul"; Harcourt Brace Jovanovich, Inc. for Carl Sandburg's essay on Lincoln at Gettysburg and "Scrapers of the Deep Winds"; University of Pittsburgh Press for Thomas Wolfe's "Gulping the Great West" (©1967 by Paul Gitlin, Administrator, C.T.A.); Alfred A. Knopf, Inc. for Wallace Stegner's "The Marks of Human Passage"; *Fortune* magazine for Bernard De Voto's "Footlose in Democracy" (©1947 Time Inc. All rights reserved).

Contents

Foreword

by John L. Bryant, Jr.
President, National Park Foundation

WHEN I was first approached about the possibility of the National Park Foundation doing an anthology on the parks, I wasn't quite sure what to expect. After all, the very idea sounded faintly academic. The anthologies I remember from college hefted like lead bars and had equally weighty titles, things like *Every Important Poem Ever Written* or *Perspectives on the Meaning of Civilization*. I wondered if any reasonably short, reasonably un-hefty collection of writings could reflect the experiences of the wide assortment of people who fall under the label "national park visitor."

So I got together with the publisher, Frederick R. Rinehart, and the editor, David Harmon, and kicked the idea around awhile. We knew there was a wealth of writing about specific parks, or the parks in general. But why be limited to that? What about all those writers who described places which eventually became part of the National Park System, but only much later? What about Charles Dickens on the Industrial Revolution in Lowell, or Abraham Lincoln on the battle at Gettysburg, or Mark Twain on the beauty of Hawaii's volcanoes? We ended up deciding that these insights were too good to pass up, even though it stretches the truth of the book's subtitle to call them "encounters with national parks."

I think it's valuable to include famous writers not normally associated with the parks because it gives the book variety, and variety, in turn, is the hallmark of the whole National Park System. Moreover, it fits right in with the goals of the National Park Foundation, because fostering the diversity of the national parks is what our organization

is all about. The Foundation was chartered by Congress in 1967 to encourage public support of the System and the National Park Service. This book is typical of the Foundation's multi-faceted approach toward its mission of service to and education for park visitors. Over the years, the Foundation has purchased vulnerable tracts of land and threatened historic buildings to hold in trust until they could be officially added to the System. It has co-sponsored a national "Arts for the Parks" painting competition. It has supervised the rehabilitation of visitor lodges and overnight accommodations in several parks. It organized the largest traveling exhibition of landscape photography of the national parks. It has produced movies, and has published five editions of *The Complete Guide to America's National Parks*. And the list goes on and on.

The Foundation's board is chaired by the Secretary of the Interior. The secretary of the board is the Director of the National Park Service. All other board members are private citizens appointed by the Secretary of the Interior for six-year terms. The Foundation doesn't receive any government funding. Being supported entirely by private sources enables the Foundation to concentrate on long-range aims that cannot always be accommodated within the year-to-year perspective of the federal budget process. The Foundation is a non-partisan, non-membership organization, though support and donations are always welcome. Indeed, all profits from the sale of this book will be used to support the national parks through the Foundation's activities.

Rather than give you yet another picture book about the parks, we at the Foundation hope *Mirror of America* will serve as a new way to illuminate and enhance your understanding of the best of our national heritage. More personally, I hope the book will inspire you to get out and see more of the national parks. When you do, you'll be in pretty select company: try Dickens, Lincoln, and Mark Twain for starters.

Preface

SOME FORTY years ago, in another preface to another anthology, Joseph Wood Krutch tried to define what makes modern nature writing different from the Classical or Romantic feeling for nature. Henry David Thoreau was his benchmark. Thoreau's work wasn't like Vergil's and it wasn't like Wordsworth's. What made it new, Krutch thought, what made it the originator of the "recognizable genre of belles-lettres" which we call "nature writing," was the author's insistence on looking at the natural world from a point of view common to all forms of life, rather than one shaped by his own desires and purposes. Thoreau was able to conceive a world where being human doesn't mean being superior to other living things, or even being unique. This made him nothing less than an insurgent—after all, his world threatened that of most western thinkers, for whom the first implication of our earthly existence is that we are the center of all existence on earth.

Not long after Thoreau died, far to the west a young Scottish immigrant named John Muir began taking long, solitary walking tours. On these walks, entirely on his own, he arrived at the same point of view as had the man from Concord. Later Muir went to live in the Yosemite, and there first read *Walden*. From then on Thoreau was his favorite writer.

If these two men have best expressed in words the idea that humans are part of a fellowship which includes the natural world, then the national parks have come closest to giving the idea its physical expression. The national parks are, like the writings of Thoreau and Muir, an exercise in humility. If we care to, we can bend nature to our will or rework history; we do it all the time. But in a few places we have consented not to. Why? What good is it to preserve natural areas and historic sites?

For one thing, by denying ourselves that which we could easily do—say, building highways all through the Everglades, or turning the grounds of Valley Forge into a monument of self-congratulation—we create, in the form of national parks, a reminder of our rightful place *within* nature and history. The parks are a perceptible reminder that we will always have some things left to learn. The national park idea is simply this: there are a few places whose qualities are so outstanding that they are worth preserving from undue human intervention because, through our act of self-restraint, these places realize their capacity to enlighten us about ourselves. So the national parks do not exist merely to let us conveniently dispose of our idle hours, and still less to provide an escape from the indignities of everyday life. When the parks are at their best, we come away from them wiser and uplifted.

That is the idea in its purest form. In reality, politics intrudes on purity, and the parks are far from always being at their best. The failures have been many, and official activity in the parks may at times seem well removed from what Thoreau or Muir would wish. But nowhere else in the history of American government has their idea been countenanced so consistently.

Krutch made a long essay out of his preface to *Great American Nature Writing* to show that Thoreau was heir to many revolutions in the realms of science, philosophy, and sensibility. Yet Thoreau was unprecedented because, having to answer to no one, he was able to imagine a wholly new form of democracy—an ultimate democracy—which proclaims for *all* living things the right to life, liberty, and the pursuit of happiness. The parks and the Park Service, in contrast, are called every day and have to answer, and so are constantly being bent and twisted by a real democratic process. The analogy between the idea that Thoreau and Muir shared and the national park idea as it exists in reality may be less than perfect. Nevertheless, the two ideas have the same essence.

The national parks are, in their compound of idealism and commercialism, of etched solitude and infuriating crowds, a thoroughgoing democratic institution, a mirror of America. Surely they reflect the Americans who made them, and so are, as Rudyard Kipling thought, at least part "wild advertisement, gas, bunkum, blow, anything you please beyond the bounds of common sense." But one can confidently say, along with Bernard De Voto, that the best part of the parks preserves "the one in the many, eternity moving through forms of change, the flowing away at once of time and earth."

This anthology gathers accounts by literate people of their experience with national parks, or places that later became national parks. Most, but not all, were written by authors whose profession was or is literary work; of them, only Muir and Burroughs can be called "nature writers." By concentrating on authors not normally associated with conservationism, I hope the reader will be offered a more ecumenical perspective. For the same reason, no person who was professionally involved with the parks is represented here. So otherwise worthy writers such as Stephen Tyng Mather, Robert Sterling Yard, and Horace Albright have been excluded.

I have intentionally left off in the mid-1950s, the time of the Echo Park dam controversy. This seemed a logical stopping point, because the overwhelming defeat of the dam proposal marked a sea-change in the history of the parks movement: after Echo Park, conservationists became more confident, more belligerent, more sophisticated. Many of the crucial issues facing the parks today—chemical pollution, intense visitor pressure on areas intended as wilderness, intrusions into the ambience of historic sites, and inappropriate development on park borders, to name a few—were unheard of or considered unimportant in the 1950s. Relations between the Park Service, the rest of the government, and the public are completely different now. I'm sure another anthology could easily be made just from the national parks writing which dates from the last thirty years—one whose tone would be very different from that of the present book.

It will be evident, then, that this is far from a collection of nature writing. Nor can it make any claim to being representative of the national parks as a whole. There is a bias here, as throughout all the national park literature (if such a thing can be acknowledged), in favor of the famous parks of the West. While there is little use in apologizing for this, the reader should be aware that this book does not do justice to the diversity of today's National Park System, which encompasses well over 300 units scattered from Maine to Guam, and from the Virgin Islands to Alaska.

So what you hold is a volume of encounters. There are trysts, rendezvous, skirmishes, and showdowns with the national parks, each according to the author's temperament. This is a process every park visitor shares in. Few of us who have been to Kilauea can express our feelings as well as Mark Twain, but all of us who have been to the parks are part of a kinship of responders, and the cumulative force of these responses, most of them favorable, should not be underestimated. The accretion, over the years, of millions of good encounters is the basis for the popularity of the parks among the American public today.

It is our bad luck that Thoreau didn't live to see Yosemite, but his mentor Ralph Waldo Emerson did, in the company of John Muir. The tone of the encounters presented here ranges from Muir's mellowish remembrance of that meeting to Bernard De Voto's acid-tinged peroration on the function of the national parks in a democracy. Since these are the bounds of the encounters, I've used them to form the bounds of the book: Muir opens it, and De Voto closes.

Putting together an anthology requires corrupting another's work, so some brief explaining of my editorial choice is in order. I kept each author's spelling and punctuation as it appeared in the source edition I used, which, for the sake of convenience, wasn't always the first edition. Except for the poems, Lincoln's address, and a couple of other pieces, every selection is an abridgment. While not wishing to burden anyone with a scholarly procession of ellipsis points, I have so indicated places where I altered the internal structure of sentences and paragraphs. I did, however, omit ellipsis points wherever whole paragraphs were dropped. Scrupulous readers can figure out what has been cut and stitched by consulting the sources, listed at the back of the book. There are glosses of potentially unfamiliar references at the end of the book as well, but I made no attempt to explain literary or historical allusions that readers can readily look up themselves.

David Harmon

John Muir

PROLOGUE: A MEETING
IN THE VALLEY

Muir first saw the Yosemite Valley in 1869. Over the years he accompanied many famous people there, including Robert Underwood Johnson, John Burroughs, and Theodore Roosevelt. But he was still a young, unformed man in May 1871 when he spent several days with Ralph Waldo Emerson in Yosemite.

They almost didn't meet. Muir could not summon the courage to introduce himself until he learned that the great man planned to leave the Valley soon. Quickly he wrote a letter of invitation, steeped in earnestness—the essential quality of Muir's character. Emerson responded and stayed on awhile. Their time together Muir later recalled in a chapter of Our National Parks.

To see and talk with a man who believed spiritual truths underlie all natural facts, and who had made that belief palpable to the skeptical world of American letters, had a profound effect on Muir, though he eventually found himself dissenting from many of Emerson's insights. Ultimately, the difference between the two men, as one of Muir's biographers has pointed out, is that Emerson judged nature on human terms, while Muir judged humans on nature's.

Yosemite Valley
Monday night

M^r R W Emerson

Dear Sir I rec'd to-day a letter from Mrs Prof E Carr of Oakland Cal stating that you were in the Valley & that she expected to see you on your return Also she promised that she would write you here & send you to me. I was delighted at the thought of meeting you but have just learned that you contemplate leaving the Valley in a day or two

Now Mr Emerson I do most cordially protest against your going away so soon, & so also I am sure do all your instincts & affinities I trust that you will not "outweary their yearnings" Do not thus drift away with the mob while the spirits of these rocks & waters hail you after long waiting as their kinsman & persuade you to closer communion

But now if Fate or one of those mongrel & misshapen organizations called parties compel you to leave for the present, I shall hope for some other fullness of time to come for you.

If you will call at Mr Hutchings mill I will give you as many of Yosemite & high Sierra plants as you wish as specimens.

I invite you join me in a months worship with Nature in the high temples of the great Sierra Crown beyond our holy Yosemite It will cost you nothing save the time & very little of that for you will be mostly in Eternity

And now once more, in the name of Mts Dana & Gabb—of the grand glacial hieroglyphics of Tuolumne meadows & Bloody Cañon,—In th nam of a hundred glacial lakes—of a hundred glacial-daisy-gentian meadows, In the name of a hundred cascades that barbarous visitors never see, In the name of the grand upper forests of Picea amabilis & P. grandis, & in the name of all the spirit creatures of these rocks & of this whole spiritual atmosphere Do not leave us *now*

With most cordial regards I am yours in Nature

John Muir

DURING MY first years in the Sierra I was ever calling on everybody within reach to admire them, but I found no one half warm enough until Emerson came. I had read his essays, and felt sure that of all men he would best interpret the sayings of these noble mountains and trees. Nor was my faith weakened when I met him in Yosemite. He seemed as serene as a sequoia, his head in the empyrean; and forgetting his age, plans, duties, ties of every sort, I proposed an immeasurable camping trip back into the heart of the mountains. He seemed anxious to go, but considerately mentioned his party. I said: "Never mind. The mountains are calling; run away, and let plans and parties and dragging lowland duties all 'gang tapsal-teerie.' We'll go up a cañon singing your own song, 'Good-by, proud world! I'm going home,' in divine earnest. Up there lies a new heaven and a new earth; let us go to the show." But alas, it was too late,—too near the sundown of his life. The shadows were growing long, and he leaned on his friends. His party, full of indoor philosophy, failed to see the natural beauty and fullness of promise of my wild plan, and laughed at it in good-natured ignorance, as if it were necessarily amusing to imagine that Boston people might be led to accept Sierra manifestations of God at the price of rough camping. Anyhow, they would have none of it, and held Mr. Emerson to the hotels and trails.

After spending only five tourist days in Yosemite he was led away, but I saw him two days more; for I was kindly invited to go with the party as far as the Mariposa big trees. I told Mr. Emerson that I would gladly go to the sequoias with him, if he would camp in the grove. He consented heartily, and I felt sure that we would have at least one good wild memorable night around a sequoia camp-fire. Next day we rode through the magnificent forests of the Merced basin, and I kept calling his attention to the sugar pines, quoting his wood-notes, "Come listen what the pine tree saith," etc., pointing out the noblest as kings and high priests, the most eloquent and commanding preachers of all the mountain forests, stretching forth their century-old arms in benediction over the worshiping congregations crowded around them. He gazed in devout admiration, saying but little, while his fine smile faded away.

Early in the afternoon, when we reached Clark's Station, I was surprised to see the party dismount. And when I asked if we were not going up into the grove to camp they said: "No, it would never do to lie out in the night air. Mr. Emerson might take cold; and you know,

Mr. Muir, that would be a dreadful thing." In vain I urged, that only in homes and hotels were colds caught, that nobody ever was known to take cold camping in these woods, that there was not a single cough or sneeze in all the Sierra. Then I pictured the big climate-changing, inspiring fire I would make, praised the beauty and fragrance of sequoia flame, told how the great trees would stand about us transfigured in the purple light, while the stars looked down between the great domes; ending by urging them to come on and make an immortal Emerson night of it. But the house habit was not to be overcome, nor the strange dread of pure night air, though it is only cooled day air with a little dew in it. So the carpet dust and unknowable reeks were preferred. And to think of this being a Boston choice! Sad commentary on culture and the glorious transcendentalism.

Accustomed to reach whatever place I started for, I was going up the mountain alone to camp, and wait the coming of the party next day. But since Emerson was so soon to vanish, I concluded to stop with him. He hardly spoke a word all evening, yet it was a great pleasure simply to be near him, warming in the light of his face as at a fire. In the morning we rode up the trail through a noble forest of pine and fir into the famous Mariposa Grove, and stayed an hour or two, mostly in ordinary tourist fashion,—looking at the biggest giants, measuring them with a tape line, riding through prostrate fire-bored trunks, etc., though Mr. Emerson was alone occasionally, sauntering about as if under a spell. As we walked through a fine group, he quoted, "There were giants in those days," recognizing the antiquity of the race. To commemorate his visit, Mr. Galen Clark, the guardian of the grove, selected the finest of the unnamed trees and requested him to give it a name. He named it Samoset, after the New England sachem, as the best that occurred to him.

The poor bit of measured time was soon spent, and while the saddles were being adjusted I again urged Emerson to stay. "You are yourself a sequoia," I said. "Stop and get acquainted with your big brethren." But he was past his prime, and was now as a child in the hands of his affectionate but sadly civilized friends, who seemed as full of old-fashioned conformity as of bold intellectual independence. It was the afternoon of the day and the afternoon of his life, and his course was now westward down all the mountains into the sunset. The party mounted and rode away in wondrous contentment, apparently, tracing the trail through ceanothus and dogwood bushes, around the bases of the big trees, up the slope of the sequoia basin, and over the divide. I followed to the edge of the grove. Emerson lingered in the rear of the train, and when he reached the top of the ridge, after all the rest of the party were over and out of sight, he turned his horse, took off his hat and waved me a last good-by. I felt lonely, so sure had I been that Emerson of all men would be the quickest to see the mountains and sing them. Gazing awhile on the spot where he vanished, I sauntered back to the heart of the grove, made a bed of sequoia plumes and ferns by the side of the stream, gathered a store of firewood, and then walked about until sundown. The birds, robins, thrushes, warblers, etc., that had kept out of sight, came about me, now that all was quiet, and made cheer. After sundown I built a great fire, and as usual had it all to myself. And though lonesome for the first time in these forests, I quickly took heart again,—the trees had not gone to Boston, nor the birds; and as I sat by the fire, Emerson was still with me in spirit, though I never again saw him in the flesh. He sent books and wrote, cheering me on; advised me not to stay too long in solitude. Soon he hoped that my guardian angel would intimate that my probation was at a close. Then I was to roll up my herbariums, sketches, and poems (though I never knew I had any poems), and come to his house; and when I tired of him and his humble surroundings, he would show me to better people.

But there remained many a forest to wander through, many a mountain and glacier to cross, before I was to see his Wachusett and Monadnock, Boston and Concord. It was seventeen years after our parting on the Wawona ridge that I stood beside his grave under a pine tree on a hill above Sleepy Hollow. He had gone to higher Sierras, and, as I fancied, was again waving his hand in friendly recognition.

I

SETTINGS FOR HISTORY

ENCOUNTERS WITH THE PAST

THE READINGS in this section illustrate two ways of meeting with the past. The first is a public, commemorative way. Open-faced, the poet Emerson and the politician Lincoln come before the audience, say their piece, and walk off the stage. Their performances are remembered today because they did what only a few have ever done: produce a graceful public utterance which recalls a specific time in history while being suffused with timeless sentiments. It matters little that Ralph Waldo Emerson was recalling a battle of a century before, whereas Abraham Lincoln spoke among fresh graves. Both the poem and the speech are not about battles themselves, but about what their authors hoped Concord Bridge and Cemetery Ridge would come to represent in the nation's collective memory.

The second way to the past is more intimate. Everyone has a store of personal recollections which mingles fact and fancy. Few of us commit our memories to paper. When we do, the tone of the recollection varies widely. For example, the easy camaraderie of Owen Wister's remembrances of Yellowstone beckons us to join him, however briefly, in years gone by. Henry James, by contrast, seems to need no companions in discovery as he stands before Independence Hall; his imposing intellect makes history a rather coolish dominion.

Ralph Waldo Emerson

THE SHOT HEARD ROUND THE WORLD

Long before Concord, Massachusetts, became the center of 19th-century American literary life, the village was the scene of the Minute Men's victory in the opening battle of the Revolution. In 1836, Ezra Ripley, Emerson's step-grandfather, donated to the village a small plot on which to erect a granite shaft to commemorate the fighting of April 19, 1775. "Concord Hymn" was composed by Emerson for the monument's dedication the following July. At the ceremony, a "great concourse of people" heard Ripley recite the hymn that had been written by a "citizen of Concord." The poem was then sung by a choir to the tune of the Old Hundred.

Emerson didn't hear them, being away on a visit. He was there, though, at the centennial celebration of the battle in 1875 when Daniel Chester French's statue "Minute Man" was unveiled on the American side of the river. The first quatrain of Emerson's poem—already considered to be "household words"—was inscribed on the base of the sculpture. Both monument and statue are now part of Minute Man National Historical Park.

CONCORD HYMN
Sung at the Completion of the Battle Monument,
July 4, 1837

By the rude bridge that arched the flood,
   Their flag to April's breeze unfurled,
Here once the embattled farmers stood
   And fired the shot heard round the world.

The foe long since in silence slept;
   Alike the conqueror silent sleeps;
And Time the ruined bridge has swept
   Down the dark stream which seaward creeps.

On this green bank, by this soft stream,
   We set to-day a votive stone;
That memory may their deed redeem,
   When, like our sires, our sons are gone.

Spirit, that made these heroes dare
   To die, and leave their children free,
Bid Time and Nature gently spare
   The shaft we raise to them and thee.

Henry James

REFLECTED DISTINCTION

James, who had moved to England in 1876, revisited America in 1904 and 1905 after an absence of more than twenty years. He traveled up and down the eastern seaboard from Massachusetts to Florida, recounting the trip in The American Scene *(1907). The chapter on Philadelphia exemplifies James's late style: the sentences dense and inflected, each one opulent with qualifications. It is a style well-suited to discussing abstractions, such as the meaning of history.*

One of James's perennial themes, the plight of uncultured America, received a twist in his description of Philadelphia. To his mind, Philadelphia's inestimable advantage over New York or Chicago was precisely that it was a city whose culture was a fixed quantity, whose society was "filled to the brim," and which therefore was "consanguine," "serene," "seated." By virtue of that ordered culture, and its seeming inevitability, Philadelphia was the perfect setting for history. To James, the events that had been played out at Independence Hall also took on the color of predestination. Basking in the "reflected distinction" of the "pink and drab" of the Hall and its immediate surroundings, he could have no inkling that one day the government would officially recognize those same qualities. But it did in 1948, and committed these environs to the nation under the name of Independence National Historical Park.

To BE at all critically, or as we have been fond of calling it, analyti-
cally, minded—over and beyond an inherent love of the general many-
coloured picture of things—is to be subject to the superstition that
objects and places, coherently grouped, disposed for human use and
addressed to it, must have a sense of their own, a mystic meaning proper
to themselves to give out: to give out, that is, to the participant at
once so interested and so detached as to be moved to a report of the
matter. That perverse person is obliged to take it for a working theory
that the essence of almost any settled aspect of anything may be
extracted by the chemistry of criticism, and may give us its right name,
its formula, for convenient use. From the moment the critic finds himself sighing, to save trouble in a difficult case, that the cluster of appear-
ances can *have* no sense, from that moment he begins, and quite consciously, to go to pieces; it being the prime business and the high
honour of the painter of life always to *make* a sense—and to make
it most in proportion as the immediate aspects are loose or confused.
The last thing decently permitted him is to recognize incoherence—
to recognize it, that is, as baffling; though of course he may present
and portray it, in all richness, *for* incoherence. That, I think, was what
I had been mainly occupied with in New York; and I quitted so qualified a joy, under extreme stress of winter, with a certain confidence
that I should not have moved even a little of the way southward without practical relief: relief which came in fact ever so promptly, at
Philadelphia, on my feeling, unmistakably, the change of half the furni-
ture of consciousness. This change put on, immediately, the friendliest,
the handsomest aspect—supplied my intelligence on the spot with the
clear, the salient note. I mean by this, not that happy definition or
synthesis instantly came—came with the perception that character and
sense were there, only waiting to be disengaged; but that the note,
as I say, was already, within an hour, the germ of these things, and
that the whole flower, assuredly, wouldn't fail to bloom. I was in fact
sniffing up its fragrance after I had looked out for three minutes from
one of the windows of a particularly wide-fronted house and seen the
large residential square that lay before me shine in its native light. This
light, remarkably tender, I thought, for that of a winter afternoon,
matched with none other I had ever seen, and announced straight off
fifty new circumstances—an enormous number, in America, for any
prospect to promise you in contradistinction from any other. It was
not simply that, beyond a doubt, the outlook was more *méridional;*

a still deeper impression had begun to work, and, as I felt it more and more glimmer upon me, I caught myself about to jump, with a single leap, to my synthesis. I of course stayed myself in the act, for there would be too much, really, yet to come; but the perception left me, I even then felt, in possession of half the ground on which later experience would proceed. It was not too much to say, as I afterwards saw, that I had in those few illumined moments put the gist of the matter into my pocket.

Philadelphia, incontestably then, was the American city of the large type, that didn't *bristle*—just as I was afterwards to recognize in St. Louis the nearest approach to companionship with her in this respect; and to recognize in Chicago, I may parenthetically add, the most complete divergence. It was not only, moreover, at the ample, tranquil window there, that Philadelphia *didn't* "bristle" (by the record of my moment) but that she essentially couldn't and wouldn't ever; that no movement or process could be thought of, in fine, as more foreign to her genius. . . .

. . . Philadelphia, manifestly, was beyond any other American city, a *society,* and was going to show as much, as a thoroughly confirmed and settled one—which fact became the key, precisely, to its extension on one plane, and to its having no pretext for bristling. Human groups that discriminate in their own favour do, one remembers, in general, bristle; but that is only when they have not been really successful, when they have not been able to discriminate enough, when they are not, like Philadelphia, settled and confirmed and content. It would clearly be impossible not to regard the place before me as possessed of this secret of serenity to a degree elsewhere—at least among ourselves—unrivalled. The basis of the advantage, the terms of the secret, would be still to make out—which was precisely the high interest; and I was afterwards to be justified of my conviction by the multiplication of my lights.

New York, in that sense, had appeared to me then not a society at all, and it was rudimentary that Chicago would be still one less; neither of them, as a human group, having been able to discriminate in its own favour with anything like such success. The proof of that would be, obviously, in one's so easily imputing to them alteration, extension, development; a change somehow unimaginable in the case of Philadelphia, which was a fixed quantity and filled to the brim, one felt—and wasn't that really to be a part of the charm?—the measure of her possibility. Boston even was thinkable as subject to mutation; had I not in fact just seemed to myself to catch her in the almost uncanny inconsequence of change? There had been for Boston the old epigram that she wasn't a place, but a state of mind; and that might remain, since we know how frequently states of mind alter. Philadelphia then wasn't a place, but a state of consanguinity, which is an absolute final condition. She had arrived at it, with nothing in the world left to bristle for, or against; whereas New York, and above all Chicago, were only, and most precariously, on the way to it, and indeed, having started too late, would probably never arrive. There were, for them, interferences and complications; they knew, and would yet know, other conditions, perhaps other beatitudes; only the beatitude I speak of—that of being, in the composed sense, a society—was lost to them forever. Philadelphia, without complications or interferences, enjoyed it in particular through having begun to invoke it in time. And now she had nothing more to invoke; she had everything; her *cadres* were full; her imagination was at peace. This, exactly again, would be the reason of the bristling of the other places: the *cadres* of New York, Chicago, Boston, being as to a third of them empty and as to another third objectionably filled—with much consequent straining, reaching, heaving, both to attain and to eject. What makes a society was thus, more than anything else, the number of organic social relations it represents; by which logic Philadelphia would represent nothing *but* organic social relations. The degrees of consanguinity were the *cadres;* every one of them was full; it was a society in which every individual was as many times over cousin, uncle, aunt, niece, and so on through the list, as poor human nature is susceptible of being. These degrees are, when one reflects, the only really organic social relations, and when they are all there for every one the scheme of security, in a community, has been worked out. Philadelphia, in other words, would not only be a family, she would be a "happy" one, and a probable proof that the happiness comes as a matter of course if the family but be large enough. Consanguinity provides the marks and features, the type and tone and ease, the common knowledge and the common consciousness, but number would be required to make these things social. Number, accordingly, for her perfection, was what Philadelphia would have—it having been clear to me still, in my charming Club and at my illuminating window, that she couldn't *not* be perfect. She would be, of all goodly villages, the very goodliest, probably, in the world; the very largest, and flattest, and smoothest, and most rounded and complete.

But why do I talk of the new generations, or at any rate of the abyss in them that may seem here and there beyond one's shallow sounding, when, all the while, at the back of my head, hovers the image in the guise of which antiquity in Philadelphia looks most seated and most interesting? Nowhere throughout the country, I think, unless it be perchance at Mount Vernon, does our historic past so enjoy the felicity of an "important" concrete illustration. It survives there in visible form as it nowhere else survives, and one can doubtless scarce think too largely of what its mere felicity of presence, in these conditions, has done, and continues, and will continue, to do for the place at large. It may seem witless enough, at this time of day, to arrive from Pennsylvania with "news" of the old State House, and my news, I can only recognize, began but with being news for myself—in which character it quite shamelessly pretended to both freshness and brilliancy. Why *shouldn't* it have been charming, the high roof under which the Declaration of Independence had been signed?—that was of course a question that might from the first have been asked of me, and with no better answer in wait for it than that, after all, it might just have happened, in the particular conditions, not to be; or else that, in general, one is allowed a margin, on the spot, for the direct sense of consecrated air, for that communication of its spirit which, in proportion as the spirit has been great, withholds itself, shyly and nobly, from any mere forecast. This it is exactly that, by good fortune, keeps up the sanctity of shrines and the lessons of history, to say nothing of the freshness of individual sensibility and the general continuity of things. There is positively nothing of Independence Hall, of its fine old Georgian amplitude and decency, its large serenity and symmetry of pink and drab, and its actual emphasis of detachment from the vulgar brush of things, that is *not* charming; and there is nothing, the city through, that doesn't receive a mild sidelight, that of a reflected interest, from its neighbourhood.

This element of the reflected interest, and more particularly of the reflected distinction, is for the most part, on the American scene, the missed interest—despite the ingenuities of wealth and industry and "energy" that strain so touchingly often, and even to grimace and contortion, somehow to supply it. One finds one's self, when it *has* happened to intervene, weighing its action to the last grain of gold.

One even puts to one's self fantastic cases, such as the question, for instance, of what might, what might *not* have happened if poor dear reckless New York had been so distinguished or so blest—with the bad conscience she is too intelligent not to have, her power to be now and then ashamed of her "form," lodged, after all, somewhere in her interminable boots. One has of course to suppress there the prompt conviction that the blessing—that of the possession of an historical monument of the first order—would long since have been replaced by the higher advantage of a row of sky-scrapers yielding rents; yet the imagination none the less dallies with the fond vision of some respect somehow instilled, some deference somehow suggested, some revelation of the possibilities of a public *tenue* somehow effected. Fascinating in fact to speculate a little as to what a New York held in respect by something or other, some power not of the purse, might have become. It is bad, ever, for lusty youth, especially with a command of means, to grow up without knowing at least one "nice family"—if the family be not priggish; and this is the danger that the young Philadelphia, with its eyes on the superior connection I am speaking of, was enabled to escape. The charming old pink and drab heritage of the great time was to be the superior connection, playing, for the education of the place, the part of the nice family. Socially, morally, even aesthetically, the place was to be thus more or less inevitably built round it; but for which good fortune who knows if even Philadelphia too might have not been vulgar? One meets throughout the land enough instances of the opposite luck—the situation of immense and "successful" communities that have lacked, originally, anything "first rate," as they might themselves put it, to be built round; anything better, that is, than some profitable hole in the earth, some confluence of rivers or command of lakes or railroads: and one sees how, though this deficiency may not have made itself felt at first, it has inexorably loomed larger and larger, the drawback of it growing all the while with the growth of the place. Our sense of such predicaments, for the gatherings of men, comes back, I think, and with an intensity of interest, to our sense of the way the human imagination absolutely declines everywhere to go to sleep without some apology at least for a supper. The collective consciousness, in however empty an air, gasps for a relation, as intimate as possible, to something superior, something as central as possible, from which it may more or less have proceeded and round which its life may revolve—and its dim desire is always, I think, to do it justice, that this object or presence shall have had as much as possible an heroic or romantic association. But the difficulty is that in these later times, among other such aggregations, the heroic and romantic elements, even under the earliest rude stress, have been all too tragically obscure, belonged to smothered, unwritten, almost unconscious private history: so that the central something, the social *point de repère,* has had to be extemporized rather pitifully after the fact, and made to consist of the biggest hotel or the biggest common school, the biggest factory, the biggest newspaper office, or, for climax of desperation, the house of the biggest billionaire. These are the values resorted to in default of higher, for with *some* coloured rag or other the general imagination, snatching its chance, must dress its doll.

As a real, a moral value, to the general mind, at all events, and not as a trumped-up one, I saw the lucky legacy of the past, at Philadelphia, operate; though I admit that these are, at best, for the mooning observer, matters of appreciation, mysteries of his own sensibility. Such an observer has early to perceive, and to conclude on it once for all, that there will be little for him in the American scene unless he be ready, anywhere, everywhere, to read "into" it as much as he reads out. It is at its best for him when most open to that friendly penetration, and not at its best, I judge, when practically most closed to it. And yet how can I pretend to be able to say, under this discrimination, what was better and what was worse in Independence Hall?—to say how far the charming facts struck me as going of themselves, or where the imagination (perhaps on this sole patch of ground, by exception, a meddler "not wanted anyhow") took them up to carry them further. I am reduced doubtless to the comparative sophism of making my better sense here consist but of my fine sense of the fine interior of the building. One sees them immediately as "good," delightfully good, on architectural and scenic lines, these large, high, wainscoted chambers, as good as any could thinkably have been at the time; embracing what was to be done in them with such a noble congruity (which in all the conditions they might readily have failed of, though they were no mere tent pitched for the purpose) that the historic imagination, reascending the centuries, almost catches them in the act of directly suggesting the celebrated *coup.* One fancies, under the high ceiling and before the great embrasured window-sashes of the principal room, some clever man of the period, after a long look round, taking the hint. "*What* an admirable place for a Declaration of something! What could one here—what *couldn't* one really declare?" And then after a moment: "I say, why not our Independence?—capital thing always to declare, and before any one gets in with anything tactless. You'll see that the fortune of the place will be made." It really takes some such frivolous fancy as that to represent with proper extravagance the reflection irresistibly rising there and that it yet would seem pedantic to express with solemnity: the sense, namely, of our beautiful escape in not having had to "declare" in any way meanly, of our good fortune in having found half the occasion made to our hand.

High occasions consist of many things, and it was extraordinary luck for our great date that not one of these, even as to surface and appearance, should have been wanting. There might easily have been traps laid for us by some of the inferior places, but I am convinced (and more completely than of anything else in the whole connection) that the genius of historic decency would have kept us enslaved rather than have seen us committed to one of those. In that light, for the intelligent pilgrim, the Philadelphia monument becomes, under his tread, under the touch of his hand and the echo of his voice, the very prize, the sacred thing itself, contended for and gained; so that its quality, in fine, is irresistible and its dignity not to be uttered. I was so conscious, for myself, I confess, of the intensity of this perception, that I dip deep into the whole remembrance without touching bottom; by which I mean that I grope, reminiscentially, in the full basin of the general experience of the spot without bringing up a detail. Distinct to me only the way its character, so clear and yet so ample, everywhere hangs together and keeps itself up; distinct to me only the large sense, in halls and spreading staircase and long-drawn upper gallery, of one of those rare precincts of the past against which the present has kept beating in vain. The present comes in and stamps about and very stertorously breathes, but its sounds are as naught the next moment; it is as if one felt there that the grandparent, reserved, irresponsive now, and having spoken his word, in his finest manner, once for all, must have long ago had enough of the exuberance of the young grandson's modernity. But of course the great impression is that of the persistent actuality of the so auspicious room in which the Signers saw their tossing ship into port. The lapse of time here, extraordinarily, has sprung no leak in the effect; it remains so robust that everything lives again, the interval drops out and we mingle in the business: the old ghosts, to our outward sensibility, still make the benches creak as they free their full coat-skirts for sitting down; still make the temperature rise, the pens scratch, the papers flutter, the dust float in the large sun-shafts; we place them as they sit, watch them as they move, hear them as they speak, pity them as they ponder, know them, in fine, from the arch of their eyebrows to the shuffle of their shoes.

Owen Wister

OLD YELLOWSTONE DAYS

*W*ister was an exemplar of the Philadelphia society that so impressed Henry James—in fact, Wister's parents were acquaintances of James. Early on, Wister exhibited the artistic talents of his grandmother, Fanny Kemble, who had been one of the most popular Shakespearean actresses of her day. Once at Harvard, Wister wrote short stories for the Lampoon and had an opera produced before graduating with highest honors in 1882. One of his classmates was Theodore Roosevelt; they became lifelong friends.

Wister left Harvard for Europe, set on becoming a composer. Within a matter of months he had played one of his pieces in the presence of Franz Liszt, who praised his talent. Wister seemed well on his way when, a year later, he was called home: his father wanted him to start looking for a respectable job. While working in a bank he took up writing again, but the literary autocrat William Dean Howells rejected his first novel as being too frank. Soon thereafter Wister's health broke. His doctor sent him to Wyoming for a change of scene in 1885. For the young patient, the vast open spaces were "like Genesis." His career was set. He resolved to become a "sagebrush Kipling."

Between 1885 and 1900 Wister took fifteen trips to the West. They provided him with the material for his most important work of fiction, The

Virginian. *Published in 1902,* The Virginian *was an immediate best-seller, and continued to be popular for three generations. It is the quintessential Western novel. It established formulas (the strong, silent hero whose story comes to a climactic finish in a shoot-out with the bad guy) and even phrases ("When you call me that, smile") that are now pure Americana.*

Wyoming was the center of Wister's West, and several times he was in the Yellowstone country. In this selection, written in 1936, he looks back over a distance of five decades to recall what the park was like in its early years.

———————

IN THE American we speak now they would have called us a bum bunch of guys. But this was in 1887. I don't know what words those dusty tourists in the stagecoaches (whom we haughtily ignored) applied to us when we met them on the road; but we heard their sightseeing screams, we saw them stare and crane their tame citified necks after us. Had we been bears or bandits (I am sure some of them took us for the latter) they couldn't have broken into more excitement. The bears in 1887 mostly kept themselves out of sight; they had a justifiable distrust of human nature, at least the black bears and silver-tips had; they had not yet learned that shooting in the Park was forbidden. But bandits you might see—possibly; there had been hold-ups in the Park. And there is no doubt that the Park with some of its violent phenomena could throw some visitors into a very special state of mind; they became ready to expect anything, they were credulous to the point of distortion.

We were merely five white men and one Indian, on six horses, with eight packs, in single file, riding at a walk, perfectly harmless, and as new to the Park as were the tourists who leaped from the stagecoaches to snapshot us. Variously scattered among these United States, our cavalcade may still be enshrined in albums of photographic souvenirs. Of course we were not the sort of spectacle you are likely to see, unless the circus or rodeo comes to town. At the cañon, a well-to-do youth whose acquaintance I had made the year before at Jackson in the White Mountains, recognized me, came up, shook my hand with gratitude, and said that if a hundred dollars would help. . . . And they put us all safe and far at a side table at the Mammoth Springs, so as not to alarm the tourists. I find in my diary that my spurs jingled so boisterously upon the wooden floors in that hotel that I removed them, blushing all the while.

"... bandits you might see—possibly; there had been hold-ups in the Park."

My diary reveals to me that I had forgotten more than I recollected of that first camping trip; so novel, so vivid, so charged with adventure and delight and lusty vigor and laughter, that to think of it makes me homesick for the past—and the past comes to be the mental home of those who can look back a long way. Weeks before we had excited the tourists, or washed our underwear in a geyser, other experiences had marked that summer as a high spot among holidays. George and I had swum naked in the quiet edge of the whirlpool below Niagara Falls; we had ridden on the cowcatcher all through the mountain scenery of the Canadian Pacific (you couldn't do that now, the cowcatcher is shrunk to a mere shadow of its former self, but it's the best seat in the train for a view). We had seen Seattle as a ragged village of one lumpy street and frame houses, reached by steamers alone; a short railroad with a long title—Seattle Lake Shore and Eastern—carried lumber only, and soon terminated at a place called by humorists (I must suppose) Stuck Junction. The University, into which I wandered through a wooden gate swung shut by a chain weighted by a tin can filled with stones, matched its large name as imperfectly as the railroad. In an upper room I found a blackboard and a stuffed owl; and in this company sat a lone young woman reading *Les Misérables*. She asked me what the word in queer letters on a front page meant; and I could tell her, because Greek was required when I entered Harvard. Presently followed seven glorious days and nights in San Francisco, the High Jinks of the Bohemian Club among the great redwoods— but I am meandering; I must get back to the one red man and the five whites and the Park.

The red man was Tighee, a full-blooded Shoshone, speaking English incompletely, and seldom speaking at all. He was our huntsman. Two of the whites were cook, packer and horse wrangler; we were the other three; and in my pocket I carried a letter from General Sheridan, recommending me to all officers of the Army. Thirty-six hours in the stage from Rawlins on the railroad to Fort Washakie on the Shoshone Indian reservation brought us to our point for outfitting. Once outfitted, we started northeastward, and reached Wind River on the second day. And here goes my diary:

"This afternoon George saw about six wild geese waddling about in a stream. He was desirous to test his horse's taste for shooting, so he fired from the saddle, thereby adding one to the number of geese. Nobody hurt." I had forgotten this.

It was the Sheridan Trail we followed up Wind River. Four years before us, General Sheridan, with President Arthur and a large escort, had taken this same route. It was nothing but a trail; solitary, wild, the Divide to our left, buttes and sagebrush to our right, and the streaming river beside us. Up the river 90 miles or so, and over a low part of the Continental Divide a bit south of Two-gwo-tee Pass, and down the Gros Ventre into Jackson's Hole, after lingering and killing bear and elk on the Divide. (It was curious to ride by, in 1893, the site of that camp two miles down the Pacific side from the summit of the Divide, that place which had been our headquarters for ten days, and find the stakes we had stretched our bear hides on in 1887 still in the ground, not one missing.)

Again my diary: "Sunday, Aug. 21. Camp 10. Head of Jackson's Lake, 7 p.m. Got here last night after 32 or 33 more miles. . . . The Tetons across the lake magnificent. I hunted all day for elk with Tighee—9 till 4—in cross timber. Awful. Tracks everywhere. Only 2 elk—which I missed like a fool. Our friend the horse thief joined us yesterday. He turned out a harmless shepherd with a nice dog, who eats your supper when we are not looking."

Of course I had forgotten about missing the elk; any thoughtful man would. But why forget the dog?

And here let me pause to lay my ineffectual but heartfelt curse upon the commercial vandals who desecrated the outlet of Jackson's Lake with an ugly dam to irrigate some desert land away off in Idaho. As that lake used to be, it narrowed in a long bend by degrees, until placidly and imperceptibly it became once more the Snake River sliding out of it below as the Snake River had flowed into it above. Serenity and solitude everywhere; antelope in herds like cattle in the open spread of sagebrush between Snake and the Tetons; these rising from the dusky blur of pines to steeps of grass, slants of rock, streaks of snow like linen drying away up, and at last the far peaks. At sunset they turned lilac, and all their angles swam together in a misty blue. Just below the outlet among scattered pines near the river, an old cabin, gaping to the weather, roof going, each year a little less of a shelter, made the silence seem more silent, the past more distant, the wilderness more present. And there among the brush was a tattered legend in print: "This very fine old rum is widely known." This relic of man crashed into the quiet spell of nature not nearly so harshly as does that disgusting dam. There is more beauty in Jackson's Hole than even such a beastly thing could kill; but it has destroyed the august serenity of the lake's outlet for ever; and it has defaced and degraded the shores of the lake where once the pines grew green and dark. They stand now white skeletons, drowned by the rising level of the water.

The Sheridan trail left the lake and the river and crossed three miles of level, turned up into timber, ran through a valley of young symmetric spruce like a nursery; cold air came up to us from a stream flowing invisible in the depths of a little cañon; and by and by we descended to a flat of thick willows that brushed your knees as the trail snaked through them till you came out on Snake again, forded it, and met discipline and law at the sergeant's cabin. Our packs were packed with trophies, heads and pelts; lucky that we needed no more of these to justify our wild and predatory aspect and prove our competence with the rifle; for here we crossed the sacred line, the southern boundary (as it was then) of the Park; and all shooting must cease; we had entered the sanctuary. The sergeant sealed our rifles. We took our way into the haunted land, the domain possessed of devils, shunned by the Indians of old.

Strange how readily the American mind swallows whole the promises in a political platform, and believes so little in any other statements, unless it is those of quack medicines! Vesuvius and Aetna had been heard of in the United States, long before John Colter of the Lewis and Clark expedition came back from his wild explorations and told the people of St. Louis about the hissing and rumbling and boiling phenomena he had beheld during his wanderings in the region of the upper Yellowstone. They set him down for a liar, and as a liar he passed for a matter of fifty years. During these, James Bridger got the same reputation. There's not a doubt that other white men saw the wonders of that weird country during those fifty years. Their traces have been found. But they were Hudson Bay fur trappers, and because of the fur they kept the secret. Not until gold-seekers rushed into Montana and parties of them (in 1863) actually saw much more of the wonders than even Colter had, were his words substantiated—or they might have been had gold not so utterly obsessed the minds of these prospectors that they hardly noticed the geysers. It was in 1870, through the official reports of a special expedition, that the whole country knew and believed for the first time that the hissing and boiling, with many other strange things, were no myth—realized this too soon for vandal exploiters, like the builders of the Jackson Lake dam, to grab and spoil; for the Government took charge of the place and by law set it aside for the recreation of the people.

As we rode into it from the sergeant's cabin through jack pines and fallen timber, at a walk, "haunted" did not seem a far-fetched expression. Mud spots of odd hue and consistency were passed; one's horse went down into them deep and suddenly; once through the trees we saw a little pond steaming; stealthy, unusual smells prowled among the pines; after skirting Lewis Lake, the trail diverged from where the present road runs north across the Divide to the Thumb, and after going northwest along Shoshone Lake, went over the Divide at a rockier place, and so down the Fire Hole River through the trees toward the geysers; and my diary says:

"The Basin came in sight over the treetops below us—merely a litter of steam-jets. It might have been Lowell." Yes; the prospect suggested to my modern mind a manufacturing center in full swing. No wonder those shooting columns of steam scared the Indians of old.

The hotel at the Upper Geyser Basin was chiefly of canvas, walls and roof; and to sleep there must have made you intimately acquainted with how your neighbors were passing the night. We didn't sleep there, we camped within the trees a short ride away; but we rejoiced in the blackberry brandy we bought from the hotel clerk; it was provided to check disturbances which drinking queer water from highly chemical brooks often raised in human interiors. And we also rejoiced in a bath the soldiers had constructed in a cabin by the river. The cool river flowed into the wooden trough one way, and through another spout, which you let loose with a wooden peg, astonishingly hot water poured from a little boiling hole in the formation above the cabin, and brought your bath to the temperature you desired. Both brandy and bath were a source of rejoicing; and after emerging clean and new from the latter, the spectacle of a little gray bird, like a fat catbird, skimming along the river like a bullet and suddenly dropping below the surface where it was shallow, and walking along the bottom with its tail sticking out in the air, filled me with such elation that I forgot the geysers and watched him. Where it was deeper he would plunge wholly out of sight, run along submerged, reach a shallow place, with his tail again sticking out. Then he would take it into his head to float on top and swim. I came to know him well. In 1896 I took his photograph high among the Teton range. I was washing at the creek before breakfast. He was sitting on a stone covered with snow in the middle of the creek, singing blithely: the water ouzel.

But I do not think that anybody there rejoiced quite as utterly as a boy employed in the hotel. He must have been somewhere in his 'teens; he was like the true love in "Twelfth Night" that could sing both high and low. In calm moments he would answer you in a deep bass. In excitement, into which he periodically fell, the bass cracked to a wild treble. He would be called a bell-hop to-day; in that day no bell was there, but the boy hopped a good deal. We would be sitting tilted back, reading our mail, the tourists would have ceased talking and be lounging drowsily, the boy would be at the door, motionless as a set steel trap. Suddenly the trap would spring, the boy would catapult into the door, and in his piping treble scream out:

"Beehive's a-goin' off!"

at which every tourist instantly started from his chair, and a leaping crowd gushed out of the hotel and sprinted down over the formation to catch the Beehive at it. Beehive finally quiescent, they returned slowly, sank into chairs and exhausted silence; you could have heard a mosquito. But the steel trap was again set, sprang soon, and again the silence was pierced:

"There goes Old Faithful!"

Up and out they flew once more, watched Old Faithful, and came back to their chairs and to silence more exhausted.

Was the boy exhausted? Never. It might be the Castle, it might be the Grotto—whatever it might be, that pre-Ritz-Carlton bell-hop routed those torpid tourists from their repose to set them trooping across the formation to gape at some geyser in action, and again seek their chairs, feebler each time. Has he in his mature years ever known more joy? I doubt it.

My diary: "Friday, August 26. Washing clothes at a small geyser. . . . We steep the garment in a quiet blue pool, deep, and shaped exactly like a great calla lily, filled to the brim and some ten feet across. Then we soap and then with a pole poke it down a spluttering crevice that foams all over until it is ready to take out and dry."

Have you ever soaped a geyser? Then you know it is true. If you have not you may think I am taking advantage of your credulity. Science explains the matter; I need not. But to soap a geyser is very bad for it; disturbs its rhythm, dislocates its circulation, makes it play when it isn't due to play, has killed one important geyser, I have heard. Before 1887, and before the effect of soap on geysers was widely known, a Chinaman had set up a laundry above an unemployed and inconspicuous vent in the formation at the Upper Geyser Basin. Hot water boiled in the vent, steam rose from it day and night, and the Chinaman was happy in the thought of needing neither fire nor stove nor pots, since he had taken Mother Nature into partnership, and she would wash his linen with her own hands. A few seconds after the first bundle of soaped clothes was stirred into the vent out jumped the geyser, hissing and spitting, and away blew the roof. The Chinaman escaped. That is the story; and early in my western adventures, when what they were telling me grew very remarkable, I always said, "Let me assure you that I make it a rule to believe everything I hear."

But when they told me of a hole into which you could toss your soiled handkerchief and have it disappear and in a minute be thrown out washed, ironed, folded, and with a laundry mark, I drew the line. That Chinaman in 1887 had an establishment behind the hotel, where I saw huge unnatural cucumbers he had raised with the help of hot moisture from the bowels of the earth; but his laundry was now beside, not above, Mother Nature's boiling water. By the time I had camped several times through the Park the uncertain temper of these bubbling holes had been more generally rumored. Not far from the Mud Geyser one day, I was passing a little girl who was poking one of them about the size of a soup plate with a stick, when a loud voice, which I presume was her mother's, shouted behind me:

"Louisa, quit fooling with that thing or it'll bust!"

Why will people scrawl their silly names on the scenery? Why thus disclose to thousands who will read this evidence that you are a thoughtless ass? All very well if you wrote your name, your address, and the date on the North Pole; but why do it in some wholly accessible spot where your presence represents no daring, no endurance, nothing but the necessary cash to go there? Around the base of Old Faithful (for example) are little scoops in the formation, little shallow white saucers into which the hot water has flowed and remained. Well, beneath the water on the bottom of these saucers the names of asses were to be seen, written in pencil. I doubt if this often happens nowadays; it doesn't pay. It was a deep satisfaction to talk of vandals with Major Harris, or Captain Boutelle, or George Anderson, or Jack Pitcher, military commandants of the Park before it was turned over to the Department of the Interior. The opinions they variously expressed about those who defaced nature were to the point. And they devised punishment for the offenders before punishment was provided by law. The soldiers patrolled the places where vandalism was likely to occur. If they caught a tourist writing on the formation or breaking it off they stopped him, compelled him to efface the writing and give up the specimen. If they found a name after its writer had gone on they rode after him and brought him back to rub it out. It has happened that a man, having completed the round of the Park, has been about to take the train when his name, discovered on the formation by a soldier and telephoned to the Mammoth Springs, has led to its being duly and fittingly effaced by himself, escorted back clean across the Park. Captain Edwards (not a commandant, but on duty there in 1891) told me this:

A soldier at the Upper Basin had reported a clergyman as having broken off a bagful of formation. Edwards found him seated in the stage, about to depart from the Fountain.

"You have taken no specimens of course?"

"No."

"You give me your word as a preacher of the Gospel that you have nothing of the sort in that bag?"

"I do."

Edwards let him go.

"But why?" I asked.

"I couldn't humiliate a minister in front of the crowd."

When we returned to the Park in 1896 many changes had occurred in it since our first sight of it in 1887. The stage road now went from the Upper Basin to the Thumb, no longer (as we had gone then) from the Lower Basin up Nez Percé Creek and over the Divide by Mary's Mountain along Trout Creek in the Hayden Valley to the Yellowstone River between the Mud Geyser and the Sulphur Mountain. There you met the road between the Cañon and the Thumb; and the hotel at the Cañon could easily have been dropped whole into the great reception room of the present hotel there. Its site was not at all the same— it was about at the junction of the road to Norris; it had but one storey, and its shape reminded you of a bowling alley or a shooting gallery.

We didn't go to the Lake in 1887. I have often seen it since, and once camped and fished at the outlet for a number of days. Not much to record of that, except the occasional wormy trout—you know them by their feeble fight, their unwholesome color, and their emaciation (I believe their state is due to a parasite peculiar to the waters of the Yellowstone Lake, I never caught any elsewhere than in the Lake or the river below it) and the reprehensible conduct of the sea gulls one day: that is unforgettable. I was catching many fish and cleaning them, and the cleanings attracted some dozen gulls. They hovered in the air, swooped on the guts I cut out of each trout, gobbled them and were ready for more. There was a young gull among them, and he was never quick enough for his parents, or his uncles, or his aunts. They always got there first, sometimes only a second ahead of him, snapped it from under his callow beak, and left him sadder and sadder. At length in pity I threw a large meal close to him; he got it, made off along the shore by himself a little way, and had it partially

The Lake Hotel

swallowed, when an adult relative spied it, dashed down, dragged it out of his poor little throat, and it was gone. He acted precisely like a child of three in a parlor car. He threw his head up to the sky, beat his wings, shut his eyes, opened his beak, and bawled and bawled.

Long before 1896 the hotels were larger, and the education of the bears had begun. They were now aware that man did not shoot them and they had discovered that campers carried good things to eat. One night in 1891 our sleep was murdered by sudden loud rattling and clashing of our tin plates and other hardware. We rushed out of the tent into silence and darkness. In the morning our sugar sack lay wounded, but still with us. . . . Many years have now gone since the bears discovered the treasures that are concealed in the garbage piles behind the hotels. I walked out once in the early evening at the Lake hotel and counted twenty-one bears feasting. I saw a bear march up to a tourist and accept candy from his hand, while his wife stood at a safe distance, protesting vainly, but I think rightly. I saw the twenty-one bears suddenly cease feasting and withdraw to a short distance. Out of the trees came a true grizzly, long-snouted and ugly; and while he selected his dinner with ostentatious care and began to enjoy it, a cinnamon bear stole discreetly, as if on tip-toe, toward the meal he had left behind him. He got pretty near it, when the grizzly paused in eating and merely swung his head at him—no more than that; in a flash the cinnamon had galloped humptily-dumptily off and sat down watching. He came back presently; and the scene was re-enacted three times before I had enough of it and left; each time when the cinnamon had reached a certain point the grizzly swung his head, and this invariably sufficed. It is my notion that the cinnamon was a bit of a wag.

In these days, the Park bear has almost completed his education. His children for generations have known the way to the garbage pile. And all have learned the hour when the train of stages passes along the road through the various woods. Along the road they wait, begging; and the tourists place chocolate and other dainties in their paws and maws. They have gone on the dole. The one step remaining is for them to take charge of the hotels and expel the management.

Abraham Lincoln

THE GETTYSBURG ADDRESS

Lincoln's ten sentences, carrying to the large crowd in his sharp, treble voice, took barely five minutes of the cemetery dedication ceremonies of November 19, 1863. He followed Edward Everett, the principal speaker of the day and perhaps the foremost classical orator of his time. Everett's two-hour speech, the effort of his career, was the culmination of a life's work in public speaking. Lincoln's brevity, to some of the press assembled, seemed ludicrous in contrast: "We pass over the silly remarks of the President"; "silly, flat, and dish-watery utterances"; "Anything more dull and commonplace it would not be easy to produce." But others caught the voice true, knowing it was "from the heart to the heart." "Could the most elaborate and splendid oration be more beautiful, more touching, more inspiring, than those thrilling words of the President?" One paper simply said, "The dedicatory remarks of President Lincoln will live among the annals of man."

Some three decades later, in 1895, Gettysburg National Military Park was created. The making of the park—which adjoins the national cemetery and preserves the actual site of the battle—turned out to be a crucial step in the history of the national parks. In establishing Gettysburg, Congress for the first time used its power of condemnation to acquire private land for a public park. A railroad which owned a right-of-way through the *battleground had objected to the making of a national park, saying that it was not a legitimate "public use," and therefore Congress had no right to take away its land. The case went to the Supreme Court in 1896. The justices disagreed with the railroad, saying that Congress had every right "to preserve the land" for "the benefit of all the citizens of the country for the present and the future." That decision is a legal foundation of today's National Park System.*

Lincoln's address reminds us that the reason great national historic sites should be preserved is because they are meant to serve the citizenry—not as places of dedication to the past, but of rededication in the future. As Lincoln would have it, when each new generation of Americans encounters a Gettysburg, they should resolve to learn, fresh again, the lessons of the place. That was the purpose of memorializing Gettysburg in 1863, and it still is.

On that November day, Lincoln's eyes could sweep beyond the audience, beyond and around to "the wheat fields, the meadows, the peach orchards, long slopes of land, and five and seven miles farther the contemplative blue ridge of a low mountain range." This was how Carl Sandburg evoked the setting in his monumental biography of the president. In this selection, Lincoln's words are followed by some of Sandburg's thoughts.

FOURSCORE AND seven years ago, our fathers brought forth upon this continent a new nation, conceived in liberty and dedicated to the proposition that all men are created equal.

Now we are engaged in a great civil war, testing whether that nation—or any nation, so conceived and so dedicated—can long endure.

We are met on a great battle-field of that war. We are met to dedicate a portion of it as the final resting place of those who have given their lives that that nation might live.

It is altogether fitting and proper that we should do this.

But, in a larger sense, we cannot dedicate, we cannot consecrate, we cannot hallow, this ground. The brave men, living and dead, who struggled here, have consecrated it, far above our power to add or to detract.

The world will very little note nor long remember what we say here; but it can never forget what they did here.

It is for us, the living, rather, to be dedicated, here, to the unfinished work that they have thus far so nobly carried on. It is rather for us to be here dedicated to the great task remaining before us; that from these honored dead we take increased devotion to that cause for which they here gave the last full measure of devotion; that we here highly resolve that these dead shall not have died in vain; that the nation shall, under God, have a new birth of freedom, and that government of the people, by the people, for the people, shall not perish from the earth.

HE HAD stood that day, the world's foremost spokesman of popular government, saying that democracy was yet worth fighting for. He had spoken as one in mist who might head on deeper yet into mist. He incarnated the assurances and pretenses of popular government, implied that it could and might perish from the earth. What he meant by "a new birth of freedom" for the nation could have a thousand interpretations. The taller riddles of democracy stood up out of the address. It had the dream touch of vast and furious events epitomized for any foreteller to read what was to come. He did not assume that the drafted soldiers, substitutes, and bounty-paid privates had died willingly under Lee's shot and shell, in deliberate consecration of themselves to the Union cause. His cadences sang the ancient song that where there is freedom men have fought and sacrificed for it, and that freedom is worth men's dying for. For the first time since he became President he had on a dramatic occasion declaimed, howsoever it might be read, Jefferson's proposition which had been a slogan of the Revolutionary War—"All men are created equal"—leaving no other inference than that he regarded the Negro slave as a man. His outwardly smooth sentences were inside of them gnarled and tough with the enigmas of the American experiment.

Back at Gettysburg the blue haze of the Cumberland Mountains had dimmed till it was a blur in a nocturne. The moon was up and fell with a bland golden benevolence on the new-made graves of soldiers, on the sepulchers of old settlers, on the horse carcasses of which the onrush of war had not yet permitted removal. The *New York Herald* man walked amid them and ended the story he sent his paper: "The air, the trees, the graves are silent. Even the relic hunters are gone now. And the soldiers here never wake to the sound of reveille."

In many a country cottage over the land, a tall old clock in a quiet corner told time in a tick-tock deliberation. Whether the orchard branches hung with pink-spray blossoms or icicles of sleet, whether the outside news was seedtime or harvest, rain or drouth, births or deaths, the swing of the pendulum was right and left and right and left in a tick-tock deliberation.

The face and dial of the clock had known the eyes of a boy who listened to its tick-tock and learned to read its minute and hour hands. And the boy had seen years measured off by the swinging pendulum, and grown to man size, had gone away. And the people in the cottage knew that the clock would stand there and the boy never again come into the room and look at the clock with the query, "What is the time?"

In a row of graves of the Unidentified the boy would sleep long in the dedicated final resting-place at Gettysburg. Why he had gone away and why he would never come back had roots in some mystery of flags and drums, of national fate in which individuals sink as in a deep sea, of men swallowed and vanished in a man-made storm of smoke and steel.

The mystery deepened and moved with ancient music and inviolable consolation because a solemn Man of Authority had stood at the graves of the Unidentified and spoken the words "We cannot consecrate—we cannot hallow—this ground. The brave men, living and dead, who struggled here, have consecrated it far above our poor power to add or detract. . . . From these honored dead we take increased devotion to that cause for which they gave the last full measure of devotion."

To the backward and forward pendulum swing of a tall old clock in a quiet corner they might read those cadenced words while outside the windows the first flurry of snow blew across the orchard and down over the meadow, the beginnings of winter in a gun-metal gloaming to be later arched with a star-flung sky.

II

SCENES OF WONDER

ENCOUNTERS WITH THE PRESENT

FOR MANY people, I suspect, the past and the future cease to be (for some few, indeterminate moments at least) upon their first view of the Grand Canyon. The Canyon—with a capital C—*is,* and therefore *is* the capital-P Present. Nothing else exists, standing on the rim for the first time. Much of the world's best literature is predicated upon such all-encompassing encounters, but instead of a natural wonder, the meeting is with some part of humanity—a character, a city, an event.

There is no doubt that, "like walking for the first time into Notre Dame or the Sainte Chapelle of Paris, there is a sensory shock in seeing the redwoods, the Grand Tetons, or Mount Rainier that dazzles all but the deadest souls." And yet, as the contemporary writer Joseph L. Sax goes on to say, "the initial experience is not long sustained when it is nothing more than amazement at a stupendous visual prospect." How does one get from the sheen of amazement to the soul of wonder? It is not easy. One must have something that all good writers have: the desire to question one's self. In each of the selections in this part of the book, awe is the catalyst for introspection, and the scenes of wonder are not ends unto themselves.

Mary Roberts Rinehart

RIDE THE ROCKIES AND
SAVE YOUR SOUL

The term "writing with a purpose" could not be more aptly applied than to the beginning of Mary Roberts Rinehart's career as an author. Trained as a nurse, she took up writing in 1903 to redeem her family's finances from heavy stock market losses. Her mystery stories were an immediate and phenomenal success. Rinehart is generally credited with originating the humorous mystery novel, sometimes called the "had-I-but-known" school of writing. The continuing popularity of mysteries based on humor and ingenuity shows that Rinehart's formula is a lasting one.

Rinehart loved new places and new people; her experiences as a correspondent in Europe are reflected in some of her several travel books. With her independent cast of mind and love of the outdoors, she was inevitably drawn to the physical challenges of the great wilderness parks of the West. Besides, she was ashamed to be forever meeting Europeans who knew more of the United States than she did. "I had never been west of the Mississippi," she later told her readers in The Ladies' Home Journal, *"never slept on the ground, knew rain only as something to keep off or out of, and water mostly as something that came out of a faucet"; now, "I take a course of national park each year as some people take a course of baths or medicine."*

Not the least important thing Rinehart offered in her parks articles, aside from characteristic humor, was encouragement to women readers to follow her lead. Perhaps the main message of the following selection, taken from a long Collier's *article from 1916, is that national parks are diverse enough to be places of self-discovery for everyone.*

THERE ARE many to whom new places are only new pictures. But, after much wandering, this thing I have learned, and I wish I had learned it sooner: that travel is a matter, not only of seeing, but of doing. It is much more than that. It is a matter of new human contacts. It is not of places, but of people. What are regions but the setting for life? The desert, without its Arabs, is but the place that God forgot.

To travel, then, is to do, not only to see. To travel best is to be of the sportsmen of the road. To take a chance, and win; to feel the glow of muscles too long unused; to sleep on the ground at night and find it soft; to eat, not because it is time to eat, but because one's body is clamoring for food; to drink where every stream and river is pure and cold; to get close to the earth and see the stars—this is travel.

This is about a three-hundred-mile trip across the Rocky Mountains on horseback with Howard Eaton. It is about fishing, and cool nights around a camp fire, and long days on the trail. It is about a party of sorts, from everywhere, of men and women, old and young, experienced folk and novices, who had yielded to a desire to belong to the sportsmen of the road. And it is by way of being advice also. Your true convert must always preach.

If you are normal and philosophical; if you love your country; if you like bacon or will eat it anyhow; if you are willing to learn how little you count in the eternal scheme of things; if you are prepared, for the first day or two, to be able to locate every muscle in your body and a few extra ones that have apparently crept in and are crowding—go ride in the Rocky Mountains and save your soul.

If you are the sort that must have fresh cream in its coffee, and its steak rare, and puts its hair up in curlers at night, and likes to talk gossip in great empty places, don't go. Don't read this. Go to a moving-picture show and do your traveling.

But if you go—!

Mary Roberts Rinehart

It will not matter that you have never ridden before. The horses are safe and quiet. The Western saddle is designed to keep a cow-puncher in his seat when his rope is around an infuriated steer. Fall off! For the first day or two, dear traveler, you will have to be extracted! After that you will learn that extra swing of the right leg which clears the saddle, the slicker, a camera, night clothing, soap, towel, toothbrush, blanket, sweater, fishing rod, fly hook, comb, extra boots, and sunburn lotion, and enables you to alight in a vertical position and without jarring your spine up into your skull. Now and then the United States Government does a very wicked thing: its treatment of the Indians, for instance, and especially of the Blackfeet, in Montana. But that's another story. The point is, to offset these lapses, there are occasional

Government idealisms. Our national parks are the expression of such an ideal.

I object to the word "park," especially in connection with the particular national reserve in northwestern Montana known as Glacier Park. A park is a civilized spot, connected in all our minds with neat paths and clipped lawns. I am just old enough to remember when it meant "Keep Off the Grass" signs also, and my childhood memories of the only park I knew are inseparably connected with a one-armed policeman with a cane and an exaggerated sense of duty.

There are no "Keep Off the Grass" signs in Glacier Park, no graveled paths and clipped lawns. It is the wildest part of America. If the Government had not preserved it, it would have preserved itself. No homesteader would ever have invaded its rugged magnificence and dared its winter snows. But you and I would not have seen it.

True, so far most niggardly provision has been made. The Government offices are a two-roomed wooden cabin. The national warehouse is a barn. To keep it up, to build trails and roads, to give fire protection for its 1,400 square miles of great forest, with many millions of dollars' worth of timber, thirteen rangers are provided! Thirteen rangers, and an annual allowance of less than half of what is given to Yellowstone Park, with this difference, too, that Yellowstone Park has had money spent on it for thirty-two years while Glacier Park is in the making! It is one of the merry little jests we put over now and then. For seventy-five miles in the north of the park there is no ranger. Government property, you see, and no protection.

But no niggardliness on the part of the Government can cloud the ideal which is the *raison d'être* for Glacier Park. Here is the last stand of the Rocky Mountain sheep, the Rocky Mountain goat. Here are antelope and deer, black and grizzly bears, mountain lions, trout. . . . Here are trails that follow the old game trails along the mountainside; here are meadows of June roses, true forget-me-nots, larkspur, Indian paintbrush, fireweed—that first plant to grow after forest fires—a thousand sorts of flowers, growing beside snow fields. Here are ice and blazing sun, vile roads and trails of such beauty as to make you gasp.

A congressional committee went out to Glacier Park in 1914 and three of their machines went into the ditch. They went home and voted a little money for roads after that, out of gratitude for their lives. But they will have to vote more money, much more money, for roads. A Government mountain reserve without plenty of roads is as valuable as an automobile without gasoline.

Nevertheless—bad roads or good or none, thirteen rangers or a thousand—seen from an automobile or from a horse, Glacier Park is a good place to visit. Howard Eaton thinks so. Last July, with all of the West to draw from, he took his first party through Glacier. This year in June, with his outfit on a pack horse, he is going to investigate some new trails.

Forty-two people set out with Howard Eaton last summer to ride through Glacier Park. They were of every age, weight, and temperament. About half were women. But one thing they had in common—the philosophy of true adventure.

Howard Eaton is extremely young. He was born quite a number of years ago, but what of that? He is a boy, and he takes an annual frolic. And, because it means a corking good time, he takes people with him and puts horses under them and the fear of God in their hearts, and bacon and many other things, including beans, in their stomachs.

He has taken foreign princes and many of the great people of the earth to the tops of high mountains, and shown them grizzly bears, and their own insignificance, and at one and the same time. He is a hunter, a sportsman, and a splendid gentleman. And, because equipment is always a matter of such solicitude on the part of the novice, I shall tell you what he wears when, on his big horse, he leads his long line of riders over the trails. He wears a pair of serviceable trousers, a blue shirt, and a vest! Worn by Howard Eaton, believe me, they are real clothes. He has hunted along the Rockies from Alaska to Mexico. He probably knows Montana, Wyoming, and Idaho as well as any man in the country.

When he first went west he located in the Bad Lands. Those were "buffalo" days, and it was then that he began taking friends with him on hunting trips. At first they went as his guests. Even now they are his guests in the truest sense of the word. By their own insistence, as the parties grew larger, they determined to help defray the cost of the expeditions. Everyone who knows Howard Eaton knows that his trips are not made for profit. Probably they barely pay for themselves. It is impossible to talk to him about money. Save as a medium of exchange it does not exist for him. Life for him is twenty-four hours in the open air—half of that time in the saddle—long vistas, the trail of game, the camp fire at night, and a few hours of quiet sleep under the stars.

The rendezvous for the Eaton party last summer was at Glacier Park Station on the Great Northern Railway. Getting to that point, remote as it seemed, had been surprisingly easy—almost disappointingly easy. Was this, then, going to the borderland of civilization, to the last stronghold of the old West? Over the flat country, with inquiring prairie dogs sitting up to inspect us, the train of heavy Pullman diners and club cars moved steadily toward the purple drop curtain of the mountains. West, always west.

Now and then we stopped, and passengers got on. They brought with them something new, rather electric. It was enthusiasm. The rest, who had been Eastern and greatly bored, roused and looked out of the windows. For the newcomers were telling fairy tales, with wheat for gold and farmers as princes, and backing everything with figures. They think in bushels over rather a large part of America to-day. West, still west. The occasional cowboy silhouetted against the sky; thin range cattle; impassive Indians watching the train go by; a sawmill, and not a tree in sight over a vast horizon! Red raspberries as large as strawberries served in the diner, and trout from the mountains that seemed no nearer by midday than at dawn!

Then, at last, at twilight, Glacier Park Station, and Howard Eaton on the platform, and Old Chief Three Bears of the Blackfeet, wonderfully dressed and preserved at ninety-three.

It was rather a picturesque party. Those who had gone up from the Eaton Ranch in Wyoming—a trifle of seven hundred miles—wore their riding clothes to save luggage. Khaki was the rule, the women mostly in breeches and long coats, with high-laced shoes reaching to their knees and soft felt hats, the men in riding clothes, with sombreros and brilliant bandannas knotted about their throats. One or two had rather overdone the part and were the objects of good-natured chaffing later on by the guides and cowboys.

Off, then, to cross the Rocky Mountains—forty-two of us, and two wagons which had started early to go by road to the first camp: cowboys in chaps and jingling spurs; timorous women who eyed rather askance the blue and purple mountains back of the hotel; automobile tourists, partly curious and partly envious, who watched us off; the inevitable photographer, for whom we lined up in a semicircle, each one trying to look as if starting off on such a trip was one of the easiest things we did. And over all the bright sun, a breeze from the mountains, and a sense of such exhilaration as only altitude and the West can bring.

Then a signal to fall in. For a mile or two we went two abreast, past a village of Indian tepees, past meadows scarlet with Indian paintbrush, past—with condescension—automobile busses loaded with tourists who craned and watched. Then to the left, and off the road. The cowboys and guides were watching us. As we strung out along the trail they rode back and forth, inspecting saddles, examining stirrups, seeing that all were comfortable and safe. For even that first day we were to cross Mount Henry, and there must be no danger of saddles slipping.

Quite without warning we plunged into a rocky defile, with a small river falling in cascades. The shadow of the mountain enveloped us. The horses forded the stream and moved sedately on.

Did you ever ford a mountain stream on horseback? Do it. Ride out of the hot sun into a brawling valley. Watch your horse as he feels his way across, the stream eddying about his legs. Give him his head and let him drink lightly, skimming the very surface of the water with his delicate nostrils. Lean down and fill your own cup. How cold it is, and how clear! Uncontaminated it flows down from the snow-covered mountains overhead. It is living.

The trail began to rise to a tree-covered "bench." It twisted as it rose. Those above called cheerfully to those below. We had settled to the sedate walk of our horses, the pace of which was to take us over our long itinerary. Hardly ever was it possible, during the days that followed, to go faster than a walk. The narrow, twisting trails forbade it. Now and then a few adventurous spirits, sighting a meadow, would hold back until the others had got well ahead, and then push their horses to the easy Western lope. But such joyous occasions were rare. Up and up! The trail was safe, the grade easy. At the edge of the bench we turned and looked back. The great hotel lay below in the sunlight. Leading to it were the gleaming rails of the Great Northern Railway. We turned our horses and went on toward the snow-covered peaks ahead.

The horses moved quietly, one behind the other. As the trail rose there were occasional stops to rest them. Women who had hardly dared to look out of a third-story window found themselves on a bit of rocky shelf, with the tops of the tallest trees far below. The earth, as we had known it, was falling back. And high overhead, Howard Eaton, at the head of the procession, was sitting on his big horse silhouetted against the sky.

The first day was to be an easy one—twelve miles and camp. "Twelve miles!" said the experienced riders. "Hardly a Sunday morning canter!" But a mountain mile is a real mile. Possibly they measure from peak to peak. I do not know. I do know that we were almost six hours making that twelve miles and that for four of it we led our horses down a mountainside over a vacillating path of shale. Knees that up to that point had been fairly serviceable took to chattering. Riding boots ceased to be a matter of pride and emerged skinned and broken. The horses slid and tumbled. And luncheon receded.

Down and down! Great granite cliffs of red and blue and yellow across the valley—and no luncheon! Striped squirrels hiding in the shale—and no luncheon! A great glow of moving blood through long-stagnant vessels, deep breaths of clear mountain air, a camera dropped on the trail, a stone in a horse's foot—and no luncheon!

Two o'clock and we were down. The nervous woman who had never been on a horse before was cinching her own saddle and looking back and up. The saddle tightened, she sat down and emptied her riding boots of a few pieces of rock. Her silk stockings were in tatters. "I feel as though my knees will never meet again," she said reflectively. "But I'm so swollen with pride and joy that I could shriek."

Above the timber line we rode along bare granite slopes. Erosion had been busy here. The mighty winds that sweep the crests of the Rockies had bared the mountain breasts. Beside the trails were piled high cairns of stones so that during the winter snow the rangers might find their way about.

The rangers keep going all winter. There is much to be done. In the summer it is forest fires and outlaws. In the winter there are no forest fires, but there are poachers after mountain sheep and goats, opium smugglers, bad men from over the Canadian border. Now and then a ranger freezes to death. All summer these intrepid men on their sturdy horses go about armed with revolvers. But in the fall—snow begins early in September, sometimes even in August—they take to snowshoes. With a carbine strung to his shoulders, matches in a water-proof case, snowshoes and a package of food in his pocket, the Glacier Park ranger covers unnumbered miles, patrolling the wildest and most storm-ridden country in America. He travels alone. The imprint of a strange snowshoe on the trail rouses his suspicion. Single-handed he follows the marks in the snow. A blizzard comes. He makes a wikiup of branches, lights a small fire, and plays solitaire until the weather clears. The prey he is stalking cannot advance either. Then one day the snow ceases; the sun comes out. Over the frozen crust his snowshoes slide down great slopes with express speed. Generally he takes his man in. Sometimes the outlaw gets the drop on the ranger first and makes his escape.

The snow melts in the summer on the meadows and in the groves. But the peaks are still covered, and here and there the trail leads through a snow field. The horses venture out on it gingerly. The hot sun that blisters the face seems to make no impression on these glacierlike patches, snow on top and ice underneath. Flowers grow at their very borders. Striped squirrels and whistling marmots, much like Eastern woodchucks, run about, quite fearless, or sit up and watch the passing of the line of horses and riders, so close that they can almost be touched.

Great spaces; cool, shadowy depths in which lie blue lakes; mountainsides threaded with white, where, from some hidden lake or glacier far above, the overflow falls a thousand feet or more, and over all the great silence of the Rockies! Nerves that have been tightened for years slowly relax. There is not much talking. The horses move along slowly. The sun beats down. Some one, shading his eyes with his hand, proclaims a mountain sheep or goat on a crag overhead. The word passes back along the line. Also a thrill. Then some wretched electrical engineer or college youth or skeptical lawyer produces a pair of field glasses and announces it to be a patch of snow.

Here and there we saw "tourist goats," rocks so shaped and situated as to defy the strongest glass. The guides pointed them out and listened with silent enjoyment to the resulting acclamation. After the disillusioning discovery that they were rocks, we adopted a safe rule: nothing was a goat that did not move. Long hours were spent while our horses wandered on with loose reins, our heads lifted to that line, just above the timber, which is Goatland. And then the cry "A goat!" and the glasses, and skepticism—often undeserved.

Day after day we progressed. There were bright days and days when we rode through a steady mist of rain. Always it was worth while. What matters a little rain when there is a yellow slicker to put on and no one to care how one looks? Once, riding down a mountainside, water pouring over the rim of my old felt hat and pattering merrily on my slicker, I looked to one side to see a great grizzly raise himself from behind a tree trunk, and, standing upright, watch impassively as my horse and I proceeded. I watched him as far as I could see him. We were mutually interested. The party had gone on ahead. For a long time afterward I heard the cracking of small twigs in the heavy woods beside the trail. But I never saw him again.

It was strange to remember how little animal life, after all, there seemed to be. The vegetation was so luxuriant in the valleys. Yet beyond an occasional bear, once or twice the screaming of a mountain lion, and the gophers and the marmots, there was nothing. There were not many birds. We never saw a snake. It was too high.

Sometimes we lunched on a ledge where all the kingdoms of the earth seemed spread out before us. We sprawled on rocks, on green banks, and relaxed muscles that were weary with much climbing. There was much talk of a desultory sort. We settled many problems, but without rancor. The war was far away. Here were peace and a great contentment, food and a grassy bank, and overhead the trail called us to new vistas, new effort.

One young man was the party poet. He hit us all off sooner or later. I have the ode he wrote to me, but modesty forbids that I give it. The poet having pocketed his pad and pencil, and the amateur photographers put up their cameras, the order to start was given. The dishes were piled back in the crates and strapped to the pack horses. The ruin of the ham was wrapped up and tied on somewhere. Dark glasses were adjusted against the glare, and we were off.

Sometimes our destination towered directly overhead, up a switchback of a trail where it was necessary to divide the party into groups so that no stone dislodged by a horse need fall on some one below. Always at the head, riding calmly with keen blue eyes, that are like the eyes of aviators and sailors in that they seem to look through long distances, was Howard Eaton. Every step of the trail he tested first, he and his big horse. And I dare say many a time he drew a breath of relief when the last timid woman had reached the summit or descended a slope or forded a river and nothing untoward had happened.

There were days when we reached our camping place by mid afternoon. Then the anglers got out their rods and started out for trout. There were baths to be taken in sunny pools that looked warm and were icy cold. There were rents in riding clothes to be mended; even— whisper it—a little laundry work to be done now and then by women, some of them accustomed to the ministrations of a lady's maid at home. And there were supper and the camp fire. Charley Russell, the cowboy artist, was the camp-fire star. To repeat one of his stories would be desecration. No one but Charley Russell himself, speaking through his nose, with his magnificent head outlined against the firelight, will ever be able to tell one of his stories.

There were other good story-tellers in the party. And Howard Eaton himself could match them all. A hundred miles from a railroad, we gathered around that camp fire in the evening in a great circle. There were, you will remember, forty-two of us—no mean gathering. The pine and balsam crackled and burned, and overhead, often rising in straight walls around us for thousands of feet, the snow-capped peaks of the Continental Divide. Little by little the circle would grow smaller until at last only a dozen choice spirits remained for a midnight debauch of anecdote.

As the days went by there was a subtle change in the party. Women who had had to be helped into their saddles at the beginning of the trip swung into them easily. Waistbands were looser, eyes were clearer; we were tanned; we were calm with the large calmness of the great outdoors. And with each succeeding day the feeling of achievement grew. We were doing things and doing them without effort. To some of us the mountains had made their ancient appeal. Never again would we be clear of their call.

To those of us who felt all this it seemed that inevitably in the future would come times when cities and even civilization itself would cramp.

I have traveled a great deal. The Alps have never held this lure for me. Perhaps it is because these great mountains are my own, in my own country. Cities call—I have heard them. But there is no voice in all the world so insistent to me as the wordless call of the Rockies. I shall go back. Those who go once always hope to go back. The lure of the great free spaces is in their blood.

Rudyard Kipling

ON TOUR THROUGH
THE YELLOWSTONE

*K*ipling *first traveled America in 1889, on his way from India
to England via Japan. The Allahabad* Pioneer, *one of the larger newspapers
in the British Indian empire, paid his way in exchange for dispatches
describing the journey. The* Pioneer's *publishers were not daunted by the
prospect of buying the impressions of a twenty-three-year-old. They knew
what kind of copy they would get: lively, opinionated, provocative, columns
to titillate, but not offend, their Victorian readership.*

*They could count on Kipling because despite his youth he was a seasoned
journalist. More than that, he had already begun to win renown as the
author of tales of India, later collected as the Railway Series—stories interesting enough to distract a passenger's attention from the oppressive Indian
heat as one sat waiting and waiting for the train to move.*

*Kipling's account of the Yellowstone country surely did not disappoint.
Fully three chapters of his letters of travel (eventually gathered and published under the title* From Sea to Sea) *are given over to the park. As
Kipling started through Yellowstone—his best sarcastic manner drawn from
its scabbard—his keenest interest seemed reserved for the U.S. Army troopers
who then patrolled the park. But as the trip went on, he gradually, almost
grudgingly, allowed himself the fuller pleasures of Yellowstone's splendor.*

Gardiner, Montana—the jumping-off point for a nineteenth-century tour of Yellowstone

TO-DAY I am in Yellowstone Park, and I wish I were dead. The train halted at Cinnabar station, and we were decanted, a howling crowd of us, into stages, variously horsed, for the eight-mile drive to the first spectacle of the Park—a place called the Mammoth Hot Springs. "What means this eager, anxious throng?" I asked the driver. "You've struck one of Rayment's excursion parties—that's all—a crowd of creator-condemned fools mostly. Aren't you one of them?" "No," I said. "May I sit up here with you, great chief and man with a golden tongue? I do not know Mister Rayment. I belong to T. Cook and Son." The other person, from the quality of the material he handles, must be the son of a sea-cook. He collects masses of Down-Easters from the New England States and elsewhere and hurls them across the Continent and into the Yellowstone Park on tour. A brake-load of Cook's Continental tourists trapezing through Paris (I've seen 'em) are angels of light compared to the Rayment trippers. It is not the ghastly vulgarity, the oozing, rampant Bessemer-steel self-sufficiency and ignorance of the men that revolts me, so much as the display of these same qualities in the women-folk. I saw a new type in the coach, and all my dreams of a better and more perfect East died away. "Are these—um—persons here any sort of persons in their own places?" I asked a shepherd who appeared to be herding them.

"Why, certainly. They include very many prominent and representative citizens from seven States of the Union, and most of them are wealthy. Yes, *sir*. Representative and prominent."

We ran across bare hills on an unmetalled road under a burning sun in front of volley of playful repartee from the prominent citizens inside. It was the 4th of July. The horses had American flags in their headstalls, some of the women wore flags and colored handkerchiefs in their belts, and a young German on the box-seat with me was bewailing the loss of a box of crackers. He said he had been sent to the Continent to get his schooling and so had lost his American accent; but no Continental schooling writes German Jew all over a man's face and nose. He was a rabid American citizen—one of a very difficult class to deal with. As a general rule, praise unsparingly, and without discrimination. That keeps most men quiet: but some, if you fail to keep up a continuous stream of praise, proceed to revile the Old Country—Germans and Irish who are more Americans than the Americans are the chief offenders. This young American began to attack the English army. He had seen some of it on parade and he pitied the men in bearskins as "slaves." The citizen, by the way, has a contempt for his own army which exceeds anything you meet among the most illiberal classes in England. I admitted that our army was very poor, had done nothing, and had been nowhere. This exasperated him, for he expected an argument, and he trampled on the British Lion generally. Failing to move me, he vowed that I had no patriotism like his own. I said I had not, and further ventured that very few Englishmen had; which, when you come to think of it, is quite true. By the time he had proved conclusively that before the Prince of Wales came to the throne we should be a blethering republic, we struck a road that overhung a river, and my interest in "politics" was lost in admiration of the driver's skill as he sent his four big horses along that winding road. There was no room for any sort of accident—a shy or a swerve would have dropped us sixty feet into the roaring Gardiner River. Some of the persons in the coach remarked that the scenery was "elegant." Wherefore, even at the risk of my own life, I did urgently desire an accident and the massacre of some of the more prominent citizens. What "elegance" lies in a thousand-foot pile of honey-coloured rock, riven into peak and battlement, the highest peak definitely crowned by an eagle's nest, the eaglet peering into the gulf and screaming for his food, I could not for the life of me understand. But they speak a strange tongue.

En route we passed other carriages full of trippers, who had done their appointed five days in the Park, and yelped at us fraternally as they disappeared in clouds of red dust. When we struck the Mammoth Hot Springs Hotel—a large yellow barn—a sign-board informed us that the altitude was six thousand two hundred feet. The Park is just a howling wilderness of three thousand square miles, full of all imaginable freaks of a fiery nature. An hotel company, assisted by the Secretary of State for the Interior, appears to control it; there are hotels at all the points of interest, guide-books, stalls for the sale of minerals, and so forth, after the model of Swiss summer places.

Mammoth Hot Springs Hotel

The tourists—may their master die an evil death at the hand of a mad locomotive!—poured into that place with a joyful whoop, and, scarce washing the dust from themselves, began to celebrate the 4th of July. They called it "patriotic exercises"; elected a clergyman of their own faith as president, and, sitting on the landing of the first floor, began to make speeches and read the Declaration of Independence. The clergyman rose up and told them they were the greatest, freest, sublimest, most chivalrous, and richest people on the face of the earth, and they all said Amen. Another clergyman asserted in the words of the Declaration that all men were created equal, and equally entitled to Life, Liberty, and the pursuit of Happiness. I should like to know whether the wild and woolly West recognizes this first right as freely as the grantors intended. The clergyman then bade the world note that the tourists included representatives of seven of the New England States: whereat I felt deeply sorry for the New England States in their latter days. He opined that this running to and fro upon the earth, under the auspices of the excellent Rayment, would draw America more closely together, especially when the Westerners remembered the perils that they of the East had surmounted by rail and river. At duly appointed intervals the congregation sang "My country, 'tis of thee" to the tune of "God Save the Queen" (here they did not stand up) and the "Star-Spangled Banner" (here they did), winding up the exercise with some doggerel of their own composition to the tune of "John Brown's Body," movingly setting forth the perils before alluded to. They then adjourned to the verandahs and watched fire-crackers of the feeblest, exploding one by one, for several hours.

What amazed me was the calm with which these folks gathered together and commenced to belaud their noble selves, their country, and their "institootions" and everything else that was theirs. The language was, to these bewildered ears, wild advertisement, gas, bunkum, blow, anything you please beyond the bounds of common sense. An archangel, selling town-lots on the Glassy Sea, would have blushed to the tips of his wings to describe his property in similar terms. Then they gathered round the pastor and told him his little sermon was "perfectly glorious," really grand, sublime, and so forth, and he bridled ecclesiastically. At the end a perfectly unknown man attacked me and asked me what I thought of American patriotism. I said there was nothing like it in the Old Country. By the way, always tell an American this. It soothes him. Then said he: "Are you going to get out your letters,—your letters of naturalization?"

Rudyard Kipling

"Why?" I asked.

"I presoom you do business in this country, and make money out of it,—and it seems to me that it would be your dooty." "Sir," said I, sweetly, "there is a forgotten little island across the seas called England. It is not much bigger than the Yellowstone Park. In that island a man of your country could work, marry, make his fortune or twenty fortunes, and die. Throughout his career not one soul would ask him whether he were a British subject or a child of the Devil. Do you understand?" I think he did, because he said something about "Britishers" which wasn't complimentary.

Twice have I written this letter from end to end. Twice have I torn it up, fearing lest those across the water should say that I had gone mad on a sudden. Now we will begin for the third time quite solemnly and soberly. I have been through the Yellowstone National Park in a buggy, in the company of an adventurous old lady from Chicago and her husband, who disapproved of scenery as being "ungodly." I imagine it scared them.

We began, as you know, with the Mammoth Hot Springs. They are only a gigantic edition of those pink and white terraces not long ago destroyed by earthquake in New Zealand. At one end of the little valley in which the hotel stands the lime-laden springs that break from the pine-covered hillsides have formed a frozen cataract of white, lemon, and palest pink formation, through and over and in which water of the warmest bubbles and drips and trickles from pale-green lagoon to exquisitely fretted basin. The ground rings hollow as a kerosene-tin, and some day the Mammoth Hotel, guests and all, will sink into the caverns below and be turned into a stalactite. When I set foot on the first of the terraces, a tourist-trampled ramp of scabby grey stuff, I met a stream of iron-red hot water which ducked into a hole like a rabbit. Followed a gentle chuckle of laughter, and then a deep, exhausted sigh from nowhere in particular. Fifty feet above my head a jet of steam rose up and died out in the blue. It was worse than the boiling mountain at Myanoshita. The dirty white deposit gave place to lime whiter than snow; and I found a basin which some learned hotel-keeper has christened Cleopatra's pitcher, or Mark Antony's whisky-jug, or something equally poetical. It was made of frosted silver; it was filled with water as clear as the sky. I do not know the depth of that wonder. The eye looked down beyond grottoes and caves of beryl into an abyss that communicated directly with the central fires of earth. And the pool was in pain, so that it could not refrain from talking about it; muttering and chattering and moaning. From the lips of the lime-ledges, forty feet under water, spurts of silver bubbles would fly up and break the peace of the crystal atop. Then the whole pool would shake and grow dim, and there were noises. I removed myself only to find other pools all equally unhappy, rifts in the ground, full of running red-hot water, slippery sheets of deposit overlaid with greenish grey hot water, and here and there pit-holes dry as rifled tomb in India, dusty and waterless. Elsewhere the infernal waters had first boiled dead and then embalmed the pines and underwood, or the forest trees had taken heart and smothered up a blind formation with greenery, so that it was only by scraping the earth you could tell what fires had raged beneath. Yet the pines will win the battle in years to come, because Nature, who first forges all her work in her green smithies, has nearly finished this job, and is ready to temper it in the soft brown earth. The fires are dying down; the hotel is built where terraces have overflowed into flat wastes of deposit; the pines have taken possession of the high ground whence the terraces first started. Only the actual curve of the cataract stands clear, and it is guarded by soldiers who patrol it with loaded six-shooters, in order that the tourist may not bring up fence-rails and sink them in a pool, or chip the fretted tracery of the formations with a geological hammer, or, walking where the crust is too thin, foolishly cook himself.

I manoeuvred round those soldiers. They were cavalry in a very slovenly uniform, dark-blue blouse, and light-blue trousers unstrapped, cut spoon-shape over the boot; cartridge belt, revolver, peaked cap, and worsted gloves—black buttons! By the mercy of Allah I opened conversation with a spectacled Scot. He had served the Queen in the Marines and a Line regiment, and the "go-fever" being in his bones, had drifted to America, there to serve Uncle Sam. We sat on the edge of an extinct little pool, that under happier circumstances would have grown into a geyser, and began to discuss things generally. To us appeared yet another soldier. No need to ask his nationality or to be told that the troop called him "The Henglishman." A cockney was he, who had seen something of warfare in Egypt, and had taken his discharge from a Fusilier regiment not unknown to you.

"And how do things go?"

"Very much as you please," said they. "'There's not half the discipline here that there is in the Queen's service—not half—nor the work either, but what there is, is rough work. Why, there's a sergeant now with a black eye that one of our men gave him. They won't say anything about that, of course. Our punishments? Fines mostly, and then if you carry on too much you go to the cooler—that's the clink. Yes, sir. Horses? Oh, they're devils, these Montanna horses. Bronchos mostly. We don't slick 'em up for parade—not much. And the amount of schooling that you put into one English troop-horse would be enough for a whole squadron of these creatures. You'll meet more troopers further up the Park. Go and look at their horses and their turnouts. I fancy it'll startle you. I'm wearing a made tie and breast-pin under my blouse? Of course I am! I can wear anything I darn please. We aren't particular here. I shouldn't dare come on parade—no, nor yet fatigue duty—in this condition in the Old Country; but it don't matter here. But don't you forget, Sir, that it's taught me how to trust to myself, and my shooting irons. I don't want fifty orders to move me across the Park, and catch a poacher. Yes, they poach here. Men come in with an outfit and ponies, smuggle in a gun or two, and shoot the bison. If you interfere, they shoot at you. Then you confiscate all their outfit and their ponies. We have a pound full of them now down below. There's our Captain over yonder. Speak to him if you want to know anything special. This service isn't a patch on the Old Country's service; but you look, if it was worked up it would be just a Hell of a service. But these citizens despise us, and they put us on to road-mending, and such like. 'Nough to ruin any army."

To the Captain I addressed myself after my friends had gone. They told me that a good many American officers dressed by the French army. The Captain certainly might have been mistaken for a French officer of light cavalry, and he had more than the courtesy of a Frenchman. Yes, he had read a good deal about our Indian border warfare, and had been much struck with the likeness it bore to Red Indian warfare. I had better, when I reached the next cavalry post, scattered between two big geyser basins, introduce myself to a Captain and Lieutenant. They could show me things. He himself was devoting all his time to conserving the terraces, and surreptitiously running hot water into dried-up basins that fresh pools might form. "I get very interested in that sort of thing. It's not duty, but it's what I'm put here for." And

A trapse in the hot springs of Yellowstone National Park was the thing to do in the nineteenth century, but is strictly prohibited in the twentieth.

then he began to talk of his troop as I have heard his brethren in India talk. Such a troop! Built up carefully, and watched lovingly; "not a man that I'd wish to exchange, and, what's more, I believe not a man that would wish to leave on his own account. We're different, I believe, from the English. Your officers value the horses; we set store on the men. We train them more than we do the horses."

Next dawning, entering a buggy of fragile construction, with the old people from Chicago, I embarked on my perilous career. We ran straight up a mountain till we could see, sixty miles away, the white houses of Cook City on another mountain, and the whiplash-like trail leading thereto. The live air made me drunk. If Tom, the driver, had proposed to send the mares in a bee-line to the city, I should have assented, and so would the old lady, who chewed gum and talked about her symptoms. The tub-ended rock-dog, which is but the translated prairie-dog, broke across the road under our horses' feet, the rabbit and the chipmunk danced with fright; we heard the roar of the river, and the road went round a corner. On one side piled rock and shale, that enjoined silence for fear of a general slide-down; on the other a sheer drop, and a fool of a noisy river below. Then, apparently in the middle of the road, lest any should find driving too easy, a post of rock. Nothing beyond that save the flank of a cliff. Then my stomach departed from me, as it does when you swing, for we left the dirt, which was at least some guarantee of safety, and sailed out around the curve, and up a steep incline, on a plank-road built out from the cliff. The planks were nailed at the outer edge, and did not shift or creak very much—but enough, quite enough. That was the Golden Gate. I got my stomach back again when we trotted out to a vast upland adorned with a lake and hills. Have you ever seen an untouched land— the face of virgin Nature? It is rather a curious sight, because the hills are choked with timber that has never known an axe, and the storm has rent a way through this timber, so that a hundred thousand trees lie matted together in swathes; and, since each tree lies where it falls, you may behold trunk and branch returning to the earth whence they sprang—exactly as the body of man returns—each limb making its own little grave, the grass climbing above the bark, till at last there remains only the outline of a tree upon the rank undergrowth.

Then we drove under a cliff of obsidian, which is black glass, some two hundred feet high; and the road at its foot was made of black glass that crackled. This was no great matter, because half an hour before Tom had pulled up in the woods that we might sufficiently admire a mountain who stood all by himself, shaking with laughter or rage.

The glass cliff overlooks a lake where the beavers built a dam about a mile and a half long in a zig-zag line, as their necessities prompted. Then came the Government and strictly preserved them, and . . . they be damn impudent beasts. The old lady had hardly explained the natural history of beavers before we climbed some hills—it really didn't matter in that climate, because we could have scaled the stars—and (this mattered very much indeed) shot down a desperate, dusty slope, brakes shrieking on the wheels, the mares clicking among unseen rocks, the dust dense as a fog, and a wall of trees on either side. "How do the heavy four-horse coaches take it, Tom?" I asked, remembering that some twenty-three souls had gone that way half an hour before. "Take it on the run!" said Tom, spitting out the dust. Of course there was a sharp curve, and a bridge at the bottom, but luckily nothing met us, and we came to a wooden shanty called an hotel, in time for a crazy tiffin served by very gorgeous handmaids with very pink cheeks.

When health fails in other and more exciting pursuits, a season as "help" in one of the Yellowstone hotels will restore the frailest constitution.

Then by companies after tiffin we walked chattering to the uplands of Hell. They call it the Norris Geyser Basin on Earth. It was as though the tide of desolation had gone out, but would presently return, across innumerable acres of dazzling white geyser formation. There were no terraces here, but all other horrors. Not ten yards from the road a blast of steam shot up roaring every few seconds, a mud volcano spat filth to Heaven, streams of hot water rumbled under foot, plunged through the dead pines in steaming cataracts and died on a waste of white where green-grey, black-yellow, and pink pools roared, shouted, bubbled, or hissed as their wicked fancies prompted. By the look of the eye the place should have been frozen over. By the feel of the feet it was warm. I ventured out among the pools, carefully following tracks, but one unwary foot began to sink, a squirt of water followed, and having no desire to descend quick into Tophet I returned to the shore where the mud and the sulphur and the nameless fat ooze-vegetation of Lethe lay. But the very road rang as though built over a gulf; and besides, how was I to tell when the raving blast of steam would find its vent insufficient and blow the whole affair into Nirvana? There was a potent stench of stale eggs everywhere, and crystals of sulphur crumbled under the foot, and the glare of the sun on the white stuff was blinding. . . .

We curved the hill and entered a forest of spruces, the path serpentining between the tree-boles, the wheels running silent on immemorial mould. There was nothing alive in the forest save ourselves. Only a river was speaking angrily somewhere to the right. For miles we drove till Tom bade us alight and look at certain falls. Wherefore we stepped out of that forest and nearly fell down a cliff which guarded a tumbled river and returned demanding fresh miracles. If the water had run uphill, we should perhaps have taken more notice of it; but 'twas only a waterfall, and I really forget whether the water was warm or cold. There is a stream here called the Firehole River. It is fed by the overflow from the various geysers and basins—a warm and deadly river wherein no fish breed. I think we crossed it a few dozen times in the course of a day.

Then the sun began to sink, and there was a taste of frost about, and we went swiftly from the forest into the open, dashed across a branch of the Firehole River and found a wood shanty, even rougher than the last, at which, after a forty-mile drive, we were to dine and sleep. Half a mile from this place stood, on the banks of the Firehole River, a "beaver-lodge," and there were rumours of bears and other cheerful monsters in the woods on the hill at the back of the building.

In the cool, crisp quiet of the evening I sought that river, and found a pile of newly gnawed sticks and twigs. The beaver works with the cold-chisel, and a few clean strokes suffice to level a four-inch bole. Across the water on the far bank glimmered, with the ghastly white of peeled dead timber, the beaver-lodge—a mass of dishevelled branches. The inhabitants had dammed the stream lower down and spread it into a nice little lake. The question was would they come out for their walk before it got too dark to see. They came—blessings on their blunt muzzles, they came—as shadows come, drifting down the stream, stirring neither foot nor tail. There were three of them. One went down to investigate the state of the dam; the other two began to look for supper. There is only one thing more startling than the noiselessness of a tiger in the jungle, and that is the noiselessness of a beaver in the water. The straining ear could catch no sound whatever till they began to eat the thick green river-scudge that they call beaver-grass. I, bowed among the logs, held my breath and stared with all my eyes. They were not ten yards from me, and they would have eaten their dinner in peace so long as I had kept absolutely still. They were dear and desirable beasts, and I was just preparing to creep a step nearer when that wicked old lady from Chicago clattered down the bank, an umbrella in her hand, shrieking: "Beavers, beavers! Young man, whurr are those beavers? Good Lord! What was that now?"

The solitary watcher might have heard a pistol shot ring through the air. I wish it had killed the old lady, but it was only the beaver giving warning of danger with the slap of his tail on the water. It was exactly like the "phink" of a pistol fired with damp powder. Then there were no more beavers—not a whisker-end. The lodge, however, was there, and a beast lower than any beaver began to throw stones at it because the old lady from Chicago said: 'P'raps, if you rattle them up they'll come out. I do so want to see a beaver."

Yet it cheers me to think I have seen the beaver in his wilds. . . .

There was a maiden—a very trim maiden—who had just stepped out of one of Mr. James's novels. She owned a delightful mother and an equally delightful father, a heavy-eyed, slow-voiced man of finance. The parents thought that their daughter wanted change. She lived in New Hampshire. Accordingly, she had dragged them up to Alaska, to the Yosemite Valley, and was now returning leisurely *via* the Yellowstone just in time for the tail-end of the summer season at Saratoga. We had met once or twice before in the Park, and I had been amazed and amused at her critical commendation of the wonders that she saw. From that very resolute little mouth I received a lecture on American literature, the nature and inwardness of Washington society, the precise value of Cable's works as compared with "Uncle Remus" Harris, and a few other things that had nothing whatever to do with geysers, but were altogether delightful. Now an English maiden who had stumbled on a dust-grimed, lime-washed, sun-peeled, collarless wanderer come from and going to goodness knows where, would, her mother inciting her and her father brandishing his umbrella, have regarded him as a dissolute adventurer. Not so these delightful people from New Hampshire. They were good enough to treat me—it sounds almost incredible—as a human being, possibly respectable, probably not in immediate need of financial assistance. Papa talked pleasantly and to the point. The little maiden strove valiantly with the accent of her birth and that of her reading, and mamma smiled benignly in the background.

Balance this with a story of a young English idiot I met knocking about inside his high collars, attended by a valet. He condescended to tell me that "you can't be too careful who you talk to in these parts," and stalked on, fearing, I suppose, every minute for his social chastity. Now that man was a barbarian (I took occasion to tell him so), for he comported himself after the manner of the head-hunters of Assam, who are at perpetual feud one with another.

You will understand that these foolish tales are introduced in order to cover the fact that this pen cannot describe the glories of the Upper Geyser Basin. The evening I spent under the lee of the Castle Geyser sitting on a log with some troopers and watching a baronial keep forty feet high spouting hot water. If the Castle went off first, they said the Giantess would be quiet, and *vice versa;* and then they told tales till the moon got up and a party of campers in the woods gave us all something to eat.

Next morning Tom drove us on, promising new wonders. He pulled
up after a few miles at a clump of brushwood where an army was
drowning. I could hear the sick gasps and thumps of the men going
under, but when I broke through the brushwood the hosts had fled, and
there were only pools of pink, black, and white lime, thick as turbid
honey. They shot up a pat of mud every minute or two, choking in the
effort. It was an uncanny sight. Do you wonder that in the old days the
Indians were careful to avoid the Yellowstone? Geysers are permissible,
but mud is terrifying. The old lady from Chicago took a piece of it,
and in half an hour it died into lime-dust and blew away between her
fingers. All *maya*—illusion—you see! Then we clinked over sulphur
in crystals; there was a waterfall of boiling water; and a road across
a level park hotly contested by the beavers. Every winter they build
their dam and flood the low-lying land; every summer the dam is torn
up by the Government, and for half a mile you must plough axle-
deep in water, the willows brushing into the buggy, and little water-
ways branching off right and left. The road is the main stream—just
like the Bolan line in flood. If you turn up a byway, there is no more of
you, and the beavers work your buggy into next year's dam.

As we climbed the long path the road grew viler and viler till it
became without disguise the bed of a torrent; and just when things
were at their rockiest we emerged into a blue sapphire lake—but never
sapphire was so blue—called Mary's Lake; and that between eight and
nine thousand feet above the sea. Then came grass downs, all on a
vehement slope, so that the buggy following a new-made road ran on
to the two off-wheels mostly, till we dipped head-first into a ford,
climbed up a cliff, raced along a down, dipped again and pulled up
dishevelled at "Larry's" for lunch and an hour's rest. Only "Larry" could
have managed that school-feast tent on the lonely hillside. Need I say
that he was an Irishman? His supplies were at their lowest ebb, but
Larry enveloped us all in the golden glamour of his speech ere we
had descended, and the tent with the rude trestle-table became a palace,
the rough fare, delicacies of Delmonico, and we, the abashed recipients
of Larry's imperial bounty. It was only later that I discovered I had
paid eight shillings for tinned beef, biscuits, and beer, but on the other
hand Larry had said: "Will I go out an' kill a buffalo?" And I felt that
for me and for me alone he would have done it. Everybody else felt
that way. Good luck go with Larry!

"An' now you'll go an' wash your pocket-handkerchiefs in that beautiful hot spring round the corner," said he. "There's soap an' a washboard ready, an' 'tis not every day that ye can get hot water for nothing." He waved us large-handedly to the open downs while he put the tent to rights. There was no sense of fatigue in the body or distance in the air. Hill and dale rode on the eye-ball. I could have clutched the far-off snowy peaks by putting out my hand. Never was such maddening air. Why we should have washed pocket-handkerchiefs Larry alone knows. It appeared to be a sort of religious rite. In a little valley overhung with gay painted rocks ran a stream of velvet brown and pink. It was hot—hotter than the hand could bear—and it coloured the boulders in its course.

There was the maiden from New Hampshire, the old lady from Chicago, papa, mamma, the woman who chewed gum, and all the rest of them, gravely bending over a washboard and soap. Mysterious virtues lay in that queer stream. It turned the linen white as driven snow in five minutes, and then we lay on the grass and laughed with sheer bliss of being alive. This have I known once in Japan, once on the banks of the Columbia, what time the salmon came in and "California" howled, and once again in the Yellowstone by the light of the eyes of the maiden from New Hampshire. Four little pools lay at my elbow: one was of black water (tepid), one clear water (cold), one clear water (hot), one red water (boiling); my newly washed handkerchief covered them all. We marvelled as children marvel.

"This evening we shall do the grand cañon of the Yellowstone?" said the maiden.

"Together?" said I; and she said yes.

The sun was sinking when we heard the roar of falling waters and came to a broad river along whose banks we ran. And then—oh then! I might at a pinch describe the infernal regions, but not the other place. Be it known to you that the Yellowstone River has occasion to run through a gorge about eight miles long. To get to the bottom of the gorge it makes two leaps, one of about one hundred and twenty and the other of three hundred feet. I investigated the upper or lesser fall, which is close to the hotel. Up to that time nothing particular happens to the Yellowstone, its banks being only rocky, rather steep, and plentifully adorned with pines. At the falls it comes round a corner, green, solid, ribbed with a little foam and not more than thirty yards wide. Then it goes over still green and rather more solid than before. After

Grand Canyon of the Yellowstone

a minute or two you, sitting upon a rock directly above the drop,
begin to understand that something has occurred; that the river has
jumped a huge distance between solid cliff walls and what looks like
the gentle froth of ripples lapping the sides of the gorge below is really
the outcome of great waves. And the river yells aloud; but the cliffs
do not allow the yells to escape.

That inspection began with curiosity and finished in terror, for it seemed that the whole world was sliding in chrysolite from under my feet. I followed with the others round the corner to arrive at the brink of the cañon: we had to climb up nearly a perpendicular ascent to begin with, for the ground rises more than the river drops. Stately pine woods fringe either lip of the gorge, which is—the Gorge of the Yellowstone.

All I can say is that without warning or preparation I looked into a gulf seventeen hundred feet deep with eagles and fish-hawks circling far below. And the sides of that gulf were one wild welter of colour—crimson, emerald, cobalt, ochre, amber, honey splashed with port-wine, snow-white, vermilion, lemon, and silver-grey, in wide washes. The sides did not fall sheer, but were graven by time and water and air into monstrous heads of kings, dead chiefs, men and women of the old time. So far below that no sound of its strife could reach us, the Yellowstone River ran—a finger-wide strip of jade-green. The sunlight took these wondrous walls and gave fresh hues to those that nature had already laid there. . . . Evening crept through the pines that shadowed us, but the full glory of the day flamed in that cañon as we went out very cautiously to a jutting piece of rock—blood-red or pink it was—that overhung the deepest deeps of all. Now I know what it is to sit enthroned amid the clouds of sunset. Giddiness took away all sensation of touch or form; but the sense of blinding colour remained. When I reached the mainland again I had sworn that I had been floating. The maid from New Hampshire said no word for a very long time. She then quoted poetry, which was perhaps the best thing she could have done.

"And to think that this show-place has been going on all these days an' none of we ever saw it," said the old lady from Chicago, with an acid glance at her husband.

John Burroughs

DIVINE ABYSS

John Burroughs's literary interests were wider than most modern readers know. There can be no doubt that the Burroughs Medal, given each year to the best work in nature writing, is named well; it was Burroughs, even more than Muir, who brought the genre before the wide public and showed them how to draw the natural world into their hearts. His writings exhibit this skill even now. In his day, though, he was some-one the literary establishment willingly reckoned with. Friend and lionizer of Whitman, widely published poet, prolific philosopher of time and religion, Burroughs was someone close to the arbiters of literature—close enough, for example, to have received Oscar Wilde during his sensational American lecture tour in 1882.

Of the authors represented in this volume, the reputations of Muir and Burroughs are perhaps the most similar. Yet the two men were markedly different in their approach to nature. Muir was reverent; Burroughs, book-ish. They were great friends from the day they met in 1896. "You are a dear anyway," Burroughs wrote to Muir in 1909, "Scotch obstinacy and all, and I love you, though at times I want to punch you or thrash the ground with you." Some of Muir's playful irascibility will be evident in the follow-ing excerpt from an article Burroughs wrote for Century *in 1911.*

In MAKING the journey to the great Southwest,—Colorado, New Mexico, Arizona,—if one does not know his geology, he is pretty sure to wish he did, there is so much geology scattered over all these Southwestern landscapes crying aloud to be read. The book of earthly revelation, as shown by the great science, lies wide open in that land, as it does in few other places on the globe. Its leaves fairly flutter in the wind, and the print is so large that he who runs on the California limited may read it. Not being able to read it at all, or not taking any interest in it, is like going to Rome or Egypt or Jerusalem, knowing nothing of the history of those lands.

Erosion, erosion—one sees in the West as never before that the world is shaped by erosion. There are probably few or no landscapes in any part of the country from which thousands of feet of rocky strata have not been removed by the slow action of the rain, the frost, the wind; but on our Atlantic seaboard the evidences of it are not patent. In the East, the earth's wounds are virtually healed, but in the West they are yet raw and gaping, if not bleeding. Then there is so much color in the Western landscape, so many of the warm tints of life, that this fact seems to emphasize their newness, as if they had not yet had time to pale or fade to an ashen gray, under the effects of time, as have our older formations. Indeed, the rocks of the Southwestern region are like volumes of colored plates: not till the books are opened do we realize the splendor of the hues they hold.

Hence it is when one reaches the Grand Cañon of the Colorado, if he has kept his eyes and mind open, he is prepared to see striking and unusual things. But he cannot be fully prepared for just what he does see, no matter how many pictures of it he may have seen, or how many descriptions of it he may have read.

A friend of mine who took a lively interest in my Western trip wrote me that he wished he could have been present with his kodak when we first looked upon the Grand Cañon. Did he think he could have gotten a picture of our souls? His camera would have shown him only our silent, motionless forms as we stood transfixed by that first view of the stupendous spectacle. Words do not come readily to one's lips, or gestures to one's body, in the presence of such a scene. One of my companions said that the first thing that came into her mind was the old text, "Be still, and know that I am God." To be still on such an occasion is the easiest thing in the world, and to feel the surge of solemn and reverential emotions is equally easy—is, indeed, almost inevitable.

The immensity of the scene, its tranquillity, its order, its strange, new beauty, and the monumental character of its many forms—all these tend to beget in the beholder an attitude of silent wonder and solemn admiration. I wished at the moment that we might have been alone with the glorious spectacle, or that we might have hit upon an hour when the public had gone to dinner. The smoking and joking tourists sauntering along in apparent indifference, or sitting with their backs to the great geologic drama, annoyed me. I pity the person who can gaze upon the spectacle unmoved. Some are actually terrified by it. I was told of a strong man, an eminent lawyer from a Western city, who literally fell to the earth at the first view, and could not again be induced to look upon it. I saw a woman prone upon the ground near the brink at Hopi Point, weeping silently and long; but from what she afterward told me I know it was not from terror or sorrow, but from the overpowering gladness of the ineffable beauty and harmony of the scene. It moved her like the grandest music. Her inebriate soul could find relief only in tears.

Harriet Monroe was so wrought up by the first view that she says she had to fight against the desperate temptation to fling herself down into the soft abyss, and thus redeem the affront which the very beating of her heart had offered to the inviolable solitude. Charles Dudley Warner said of it, "I experienced for a moment an indescribable terror of nature, a confusion of mind, a fear to be alone in such a presence."

It is beautiful, oh, how beautiful! but it is a beauty that awakens a feeling of solemnity and awe. We called it the "divine abyss." It seems as much of heaven as of earth. Of the many descriptions of it, none seems adequate. To rave over it, or to pour into it a torrent of superlatives, is of little avail. My companion came nearer the mark when she quietly repeated from Revelation, "And he carried me away in the spirit of a great and high mountain, and shewed me that great city, the holy Jerusalem." It does indeed suggest a far-off, half-sacred antiquity, some greater Jerusalem, Egypt, Babylon, or India. We speak of it as a scene; it is more like a vision, so foreign is it to all other terrestrial spectacles, and so surpassingly beautiful.

To ordinary folk, the spectacle is so extraordinary, so unlike everything one's experience has yielded, and so unlike the results and the usual haphazard working of the blind forces of nature, that I did not wonder when people whom I met on the rim asked me what I supposed did all this. I could even sympathize with the remark of an old woman visitor who is reported to have said that she thought they had built the cañon too near the hotel. The enormous cleavage which the cañon shows, the abrupt drop from the brink of thousands of feet, the sheer faces of perpendicular walls of dizzy height, give at first the impression that it is all the work of some titanic quarryman, who must have removed cubic miles of strata as we remove cubic yards of earth.

Indeed, go out to O'Neil's, or Hopi, Point, and, as you emerge from the woods, you get glimpses of a blue or rose-purple gulf opening before you. The solid ground ceases suddenly, and an aerial perspective vast and alluring, takes its place; another heaven, counter-sunk in the earth, transfixes you on the brink. "Great God!" I can fancy the first beholder of it saying, "What is this? Do I behold a transfiguration of the earth? Has the solid ground melted into thin air? Is there a firmament below as well as above? Has the earth's veil at last been torn aside, and the red heart of the globe laid bare?" If this first witness was not at once overcome by the beauty of the earthly revelation before him, or terrified by its strangeness and power, he must have stood long, awed and spellbound, speechless with astonishment, and thrilled with delight. He may have seen vast and glorious prospects from mountain-tops, he may have looked down upon the earth and seen it unroll like a map before him; but he had never before looked *into* the earth as through a mighty window or open door, and beheld depths and gulfs of space, with their atmospheric veils and illusions and vast perspectives, such as he had seen from mountain-summits, but with a wealth of color and a suggestion of architectural and monumental remains, and a strange almost unearthly beauty, such as no mountain-view could ever have afforded him.

One's sense of the depths of the cañon is so great that it almost makes one dizzy to see the little birds fly out over it, or plunge down into it. One seemed to fear that they, too, would get dizzy and fall to the bottom. We watched a line of tourists on mules creeping along the trail across the inner plateau, and the unaided eye had trouble to hold them; they looked like little red ants. The eye has more difficulty in estimating objects and distances beneath it than when they are above or on a level with it, because it is so much less familiar with depth than with height or lateral dimensions.

One of the remarkable and unexpected things about the cañon is its look of ordered strength. There is no debris or loose wreckage, no tumbled confusion of fallen rocks, but the symmetry and proportion of a city or a fortress. Nearly all the lines are lines of greatest strength. . . . The simple, strong structural lines assert themselves everywhere, and give that look of repose and security characteristic of the scene. The rocky forces always seem to retreat in good order before the onslaught of time; there is neither rout nor confusion. Everywhere they present a calm, upright front to the foe. And the fallen from their ranks, where are they? A cleaner battle-field between the forces of nature one rarely sees.

The weaker portions are of course constantly giving way. The elements incessantly lay siege to these fortresses and take advantage of every flaw or unguarded point, so that what stands has been seven times, yea, seventy times seven tested, and hence gives the impression of impregnable strength. The angles and curves, the terraces and foundations, seem to be the work of some master engineer, with only here and there a toppling rock, and with no chaos or confusion anywhere.

All the litter and rubbish seems to have been cleared up, and the job finished. Indeed, such an effect of finished work in mountain and gorge I have never before seen.

During those days at the cañon how often I thought of the geology of my native hills amid the Catskills, which show the effects of denudation as much older than that shown here as this is older than the washout in the road by this morning's shower. The old red sandstone in which I hoed corn as a farm-boy dates back to middle Paleozoic time, or to the spring of the great geologic year, while the cañon is of the late autumn. Could my native hills have replied to my mute questionings, they would have said: "We were old, old, and had passed through the cañon stage long before the Grand Cañon was born. We have had all that experience, and have forgotten it ages and ages ago. No vestige of our cañons remain. They have all been worn down and obliterated by the strokes of a hand as gentle as that of a passing cloud. Where they were, are now broad, fertile valleys, with rounded knolls and gentle slopes, and the sound of peaceful husbandry. The great ice sheet rubbed us and plowed us, but our contours were gentle and rounded eons before that event. When the Grand Cañon is as old as we are, all its superb architectural features will have long since disappeared, its gigantic walls will have crumbled, and rolling plains and gentle valleys will have taken its place."

All of which seems quite probable. With time enough, the gentle forces of air and water will surely change the whole aspect of this tremendous chasm.

On the second day we made the descent into the cañon on muleback. That veteran mountain-climber and glacier-meadow Scotsman John Muir pooh-poohed the scheme. "Go up," he said, "and not down. Climb, climb; do not fancy that you can bestride a mule and go down into that hole and find the glory that lures you from the top."

But we were not to be dissuaded or ridiculed out of the adventure. There is always satisfaction in going to the bottom of things. Then, we wanted to get on more intimate terms with the great abyss, to wrestle with it, if need be, and to feel its power, as well as to behold it. It is not best always to dwell upon the rim of things or to look down upon them from afar. The summits are good, but the valleys have their charm, also; even the valley of humiliation has its lessons. At any rate, four of us were unanimous in our desire to sound that vast profound on mule-back, trusting that the return trip would satisfy our "climbing" aspirations, as it did. The sarcastic Scotsman, seeing that we were not to be ridiculed out of the adventure, reluctantly consented to be one of the misguided party.

It is quite worth while to go down into the cañon on mule-back, if only to fall in love with a mule, and to learn what a sure-footed, careful, and docile creature, when he is on his good behavior, a mule can be. My mule was named "Johnny," and there was soon a good understanding between us. I quickly learned to turn the whole problem over to him. He knew how to take the sharp turns and narrow shelves of that steep zigzag much better than I did. I do not fancy that the thought of my safety was Johnny's guiding star; his solicitude struck nearer home than that. There was much ice and snow on the upper part of the trail, and only those slender little legs of Johnny's stood between me and a tumble of two or three thousand feet. How cautiously he felt his way with his round little feet, as, with lowered head, he seemed to be scanning the trail critically! Only when he swung around the sharp elbows of the trail did his fore-feet come near the edge of the brink. Only once or twice at such times, as we hung for a breath above the terrible incline, did I feel a slight shudder. One of my companions, who had never before been upon an animal's back, so fell in love with her "Sandy" that she longed for a trunk big enough in which to take him home with her.

It was more than worth while to make the descent to traverse that Cambrian plateau, which from the rim is seen to flow out from the base of the enormous cliffs to the brink of the inner chasm, looking like some soft lavender-colored carpet or rug. I had never seen the Cambrian rocks, the lowest of the stratified formations, nor set my foot upon Cambrian soil. Hence a new experience was promised me. Rocky layers probably two or three miles thick had been worn away from the old Cambrian foundations, and when I looked down upon that gently undulating plateau, the thought of the eternity of time which it represented tended quite as much to make me dizzy as did the drop of nearly four thousand feet. We found it gravelly and desert-like, covered with cacti, low sage-brush, and other growths. The dim trail led us to its edge, where we could look down into the twelve hundred foot V-shaped gash which the river had cut into the dark, crude-looking archaean rock. How distinctly it looked like a new day in creation where the horizontal, yellowish-gray beds of the Cambrian were laid down upon the dark, amorphous, and twisted older granite! How carefully the level strata had been fitted to the shapeless mass beneath it! It all looked like the work of a master mason; apparently you could put the point of your knife where one formation ended and the other began. The older rock suggested chaos and turmoil, the other suggested order and plan, as if the builder had said, "Now upon this foundation we will build our house." It is an interesting fact, the full geologic significance of which I suppose I do not appreciate, that the different formations are usually marked off from one another in just this sharp way, as if each one was indeed the work of a separate day of creation. Nature appears at long intervals to turn over a new leaf and start a new chapter in her great book. The transition from one geologic age to another appears to be abrupt: new colors, new constituents, new qualities appear in the rocks with a suddenness hard to reconcile with Lyell's doctrine of uniformitarianism, just as new species appear in the life of the globe with an abruptness hard to reconcile with Darwin's slow process of natural selection. Is sudden mutation, after all, the key to all these phenomena?

We ate our lunch on the old Cambrian table, placed there for us so long ago, and gazed down upon the turbulent river hiding and reappearing in its labyrinthian channel so far below us.

It is worth while to make the descent in order to look upon the river which has been the chief quarryman in excavating the cañon, and to find how inadequate it looks for the work ascribed to it. Viewed from where we sat, I judged it to be forty or fifty feet broad, but I was assured that it was between two and three hundred feet. Water and sand are ever symbols of instability and inconstancy, but let them work together, and they saw through mountains, and undermine the foundations of the hills.

It is always worth while to sit or kneel at the feet of grandeur, to look up into the placid faces of the earth gods and feel their power, and the tourist who goes down into the cañon certainly has this privilege. We did not bring back in our hands, or in our hats, as the Scotsman said we could not, the glory that had lured us from the top, but we seemed to have been nearer its sources, and to have brought back a deepened sense of the magnitude of the forms, and of the depth of the chasm which we had heretofore gazed upon from a distance. Also we had plucked the flower safety from the nettle danger, always an exhilarating enterprise.

In climbing back, my eye, now sharpened by my geologic reading, dwelt frequently and long upon the horizon where that cross-bedded carboniferous sandstone joins the carboniferous limestone above it. How much older the sandstone looked! I could not avoid the impression that its surface must have formed a plane of erosion ages and ages before the limestone had been laid down upon it.

We had left plenty of ice and snow at the top, but in the bottom we found the early spring flowers blooming, and a settler at what is called the Indian gardens was planting his garden. Here I heard the song of the cañon wren, a new and very pleasing bird-song to me. I think our dreams were somewhat disturbed that night by the impressions of the day, but our day-dreams since that time have at least been sweeter and more comforting, and I am sure that the remainder of our lives will be the richer for our having seen the Grand Cañon.

Harriet Monroe

TWO POEMS

Good poetry about the national parks is hard to find. While many amateurs have taken up the topic—with overwhelmingly amateurish results—professional poets have mostly shied away, preferring to address nature in general rather than specific natural wonders. Their reasoning is plain: the grandeur embodied in the most famous national parks is a daunting subject to capture in verse. Unless handled with absolute expertness, poetic techniques can only trivialize a Yosemite Valley.

Even in the hands of an expert, there is a tendency for poetry to enshrine the parks rather than evoke them. The work of Harriet Monroe is a case in point. She became interested in the parks after a visit to the Grand Canyon in 1899; there followed many magazine articles and poems. Her style is amply illustrated by the following selections: a catalogue of the personalities of Yosemite's waterfalls, and a paean to the nearby Hetch Hetchy Valley, written during the height of the debate on whether it should be inundated by a reservoir. Even if these verses lack distinction, they are assuredly the work of a consummate professional.

Monroe's achievements as a poet may have been modest, but her name will always be remembered by students of American literature, for in 1912 she founded Poetry: A Magazine of Verse, editing it until the end of her life in 1936. Her talent was not in writing verse, but in recogniz-

ing talent in that of others. In the early years of Poetry, *she was widely acknowledged for her judicious taste in an extremely arbitrary profession. Mostly, that assessment has proved true: among the young poets whose careers were furthered by Monroe's advocacy were Rupert Brooke, Hart Crane, Robinson Jeffers, Marianne Moore, and Stephen Spender. Still published today,* Poetry *has been called the most influential journal of its kind.*

The Cataracts

The Yosemite leaps from the peaks
And plunges down deep into the valley,
Tossing the spring from his arms
To her couch of flowers.
Tall as El Capitan the mighty,
From earth to heaven he glistens like a god,
And mountain-loads of snow-waters
    foam into clouds for his feet.
In thunderous peal on peal
He shouts to all the choral fountains—
To silver-fingered Nevada the dancer,
To Vernal, her dark-browed lover,
    massive, square-shouldered,
To Illillouette the fairy, tripping in satin slippers
    down over the rocks.

In huge musical volleys he shouts to them,
And they answer in diapasons
    rolling from mountain to mountain,
And in songs feather-soft, that float away
    airily on the wind.
Rushing, yet forever still,
Tiptoeing the tall sequoias,
The cataracts crown the Summer with rainbows
As they lift crystal cups to her beauty
And chant her praise to the sun.

Yosemite Falls

The Hetch-Hetchy

Have you found the Happy Valley?
  No? Then follow—I have seen
    Where it lies.
Shoon and staff—oh, leave your alley!
  Pass the foot-hills, pass the green
    Gates that rise.

Soft it slumbers, locked in granite,
  Cliffs like silver-mailèd knights
    Ranged round.
And the mountain breezes fan it—
  Snow-plumed winds from hoary heights
    Glacier-crowned.

There slim waterfalls dash madly,
  Breaking, foaming, thundering
    As they pass
Into blue-eyed brooks that gladly
  Trail their gauzy gowns and ring
    Bells of glass.

There the Rancheria, laughing,
  Down her cleft of granite trips
    Like a girl;
Leaps to meet her lover, quaffing
  Cataracts through foamy lips
    As they whirl.

And Tuolumne the river
  From his plunges mountain-deep
    Rests awhile;
Winds with many a curve and quiver
  Down in flowery glades asleep,
    Mile on mile.

Come—'neath plumy cedars lying
  We shall hear his crystal tune
    Filmy soft;
Watch his foamy fringes flying
  Till the mountain-climbing moon
    Rides aloft.

Then the stars will guard our slumbers—
  Never head in royal bed
    Lay so still—
While the stream sings lulling numbers
  And the ghostly shadows tread
    Where they will.

Oh the golden days that shimmer
  In that deep entrancèd vale
    Richly bright!
Oh the twilights dim and dimmer
  Till the granite shoulders pale
    Falls the night!

Come, friend, pass the frowning portals!
  'T is the Magic Valley—stay—
    'T is your quest.
Come, forget that we are mortals—
  Where the gods have had their way
    Men are blest.

Carl Sandburg

SCRAPERS OF
THE DEEP WINDS

Sandburg was one of the poets to whom Monroe first gave promi-
nence. Until his appearance in Poetry, he was known only in the Midwest
and only as a journalist. Afterwards, he became one of the leaders of the
Chicago Renaissance, a group of writers whose work made the city
America's literary capital from about 1912 until the early 1920s. During
that period, Sandburg secured a national reputation, and was able to devote
himself to his favorite form of poetry: a celebration, in free verse and col-
loquial talk, of the landscape and people of the United States. In "Many
Hats," which appeared in his 1928 collection Good Morning, America,
Sandburg and his characters step up to the mythic edge of the Grand
Canyon. The language of the poem is typical of his verse.

Some seventeen years after publishing Good Morning, America, Sandburg moved to a new home, called Connemara, high on a hill in the town
of Flat Rock, North Carolina. There he lived, with the Blue Ridge in the
northern distance, until his death in 1967. This beautiful farm-estate is
now a National Historic Site. Each room of the main house is kept as
though Sandburg had just left it.

MANY HATS

1

When the scrapers of the
deep winds were done, and
the haulers of the tall
waters had finished, this
was the accomplishment.

The drums of the sun never
get tired, and first off
every morning, the drums of
the sun perform an intro-
duction of the dawn here.

The moon goes down here
as a dark bellringer doing
once more what he has done
over and over already in
his young life.

Up on a long blue platform
comes a line of starprints.
If the wind has a song, it
is moaning: Good Lawd, I
done done what you told me
to do.

2

Whose three-ring circus is this? Who stipulated in a contract for this
to be drunken, death-defying, mammoth, cyclopean, mystic as the light
that never was on land or sea, bland, composed, and imperturbable
as a cool phalanx of sphinxes? Why did one woman cry, The silence
is terrible? Why did another smile, There is a sweet gravity here? Why
do they come and go here and look as in a looking-glass?

The Grand Canyon of Arizona, said one, this is it, hacked out by
the broadax of a big left-handed God and left forgotten, fixed over
and embellished by a remembering right-handed God who always
comes back.

If you ask me, said an old railroader, I'll never tell you who took the excavation contract for this blowout—it took a lot of shovels and a lot of dynamite—several large kegs, I would guess—and maybe they had a case or two of T N T.

Yes, he went on, the Grand Canyon, the daddy of 'em all—the undisputed champeen—that range rider sure was righto—the elements had a hell of a rassle here.

The Grand Canyon—a long ride from where Brigham Young stands in bronze gazing on the city he bade rise out of salt and alkali—a weary walk from Santa Fé and the Mountains of the Blood of Christ—a bitter hike from where the Sonora dove at Tucson mourns, No hope, no hope—a sweet distance from where Balboa stripped for his first swim in the Pacific—a mean cross-country journey to where Roy Bean told the muchacho, By the white light of a moon on the walls of an arroyo last Tuesday you killed a woman and next Tuesday we're going to hang you—a traveler's route of many days and sleeps to reach the place of the declaration, God reigns and the government at Washington lives.

Shovel into this cut of earth all past and present possessions, creations, belongings of man; shovel furioso, appassionata, pizzicato; shovel cities, wagons, ships, tools, jewels; the bottom isn't covered; the wild burros and the trail mules go haw-hee, haw-hee, haw-hee.

Turn it into a Hall of Fame, said a rambler, let it be a series of memorials to the Four Horsemen, to Napoleon, Carl the Twelfth, Caesar, Alexander the Great, Hannibal and Hasdrubal, and all who have rode in blood up to the bridles of the horses, calling, Hurrah for the next who goes—let each have his name on a truncated cyclops of rock—let passers-by say, He was pretty good but he didn't last long.

Now I wonder, I wonder, said another, can they all find room here? Elijah fed by ravens, Jonah in the belly of the whale, Daniel in the lion's den, Lot's wife transmogrified into salt, Elijah riding up into the sky in a chariot of fire—can they all find room? Are the broken pieces of the Tower of Babel and the Walls of Jericho here? Should I look for the ram's horn Joshua blew?

3

A phantom runner runs on the rim. "I saw a moon man throw hats in, hats of kings, emperors, senators, presidents, plumed hats of knights, red hats of cardinals, five-gallon hats of cowboys, tasseled hats of Bavarian yodelers, mandarin hats, derbies, fedoras, chapeaus, straws, lady picture hats out of Gainsborough portraits—

"Hats many proud people handed over, dying and saying, Take this one too—hats furioso, appassionata, pizzicato—hats for remembrance, good-by, three strikes and out, fade me, there's no place to go but home—hats for man alone, God alone, the sky alone."

4

Think of the little birds, said another, the wee birdies—before God took a hunk of mud and made Man they were here, the birds, the robins, juncoes, nuthatches, bats, eagles, cedar birds, chickadees, blue-jays, I saw a blackbird gleaming in satin, floating in the scrolls of his glamorous wings, stopping on an airpath and standing still with nothing under his feet, looking at the gray Mojave desert level interrupted by the Grand Canyon—the birds belong, don't they?

5

Comes an hombre saying, Let it be dedicated to Time; this is what is left of the Big Procession when Time gets through with it; the sun loves its stubs; we will give a name to any torso broken and tumbled by Time; we will leave the vanished torsos with no names.

Comes along an hombre accidentally remarking, Let it be dedicated to Law and Order—the law of the Strong fighting the Strong, the Cunning outwitting the Less Cunning—and the Weak Ones ordered to their places by the Strong and Cunning—aye—and ai-ee—Law and Order.

Comes along another hombre giving his slant at it, Now this sure was the Gyarden of Eden, smooth, rich, nice, watered, fixed, no work till tomorrow, Adam and Eve satisfied and sitting pretty till the day of the Snake Dance and the First Sin; and God was disgusted and wrecked the works; he ordered club-foot angels with broken wings to shoot the job; now look at it.

Comes another hombre all wised up, This was the Devil's Brickyard;
here were the kilns to make the Kitchens of Hell; after bricks enough
were made to last Hell a million years, the Devil said, "Shut 'er down";
they had a big payday night and left it busted from hell to breakfast;
the Hopis looked it over and decided to live eighty miles away where
there was water; then came Powell, Hance, the Santa Fé, the boys
shooting the rapids, and Fred Harvey with El Tovar.

6

Now Hance had his points; they asked him how he come to find the Canyon and he told 'em, I was ridin' old Whitey and the Mojaves after me when we comes to this gap miles across; I told Whitey, It's you now for the longest jump you ever took; Whitey jumped and was half way across when I pulled on the bridle, turned him around, and we come back to the same place on the Canyon rim we started from.

Yes, Hance told 'em, if they asked, how he come to dig the Canyon. "But where did you put all the dirt?" "Took it away in wheelbarrows and made San Francisco Peaks."

Hance sleeping near a big rock, woke up and saw seven rattlesnakes circle seven times around the rock, each with the tail of the snake ahead in his mouth, and all of them swallowing, till after a while there wasn't a snake left. Hance's wife got her leg caught between two rocks; couldn't get her loose, said Hance, so I had to shoot her to save her from starving to death; look down there between those two rocks and you can see her bones, said Hance.

This is where we find the original knuckle snake; he breaks to pieces if you try to pick him up; and when you go away he knuckles himself together again; yes, and down here, is the original echo canyon; we holler, "Has Smith been here?" and the echo promulgates back, "Which Smith?"

7

Down at the darkest depths, miles down, the Colorado River grinds, toils, driving the channel deeper—is it free or convict?—tell me—will it end like a great writer crying, I die with my best books unwritten?

Smooth as glass run the streaming waters—then a break into rapids, into tumblers, into spray, into voices, roars, growls, into commanding monotones that hunt far corners and jumping-off places.

And how should a beautiful, ignorant stream of water know it heads for an early release—out across the desert, running toward the Gulf, below sea level, to murmur its lullaby, and see the Imperial Valley rise out of burning sand with cotton blossoms, wheat, watermelons, roses, how should it know?

8

The hombres keep coming; here comes another; he says, says he, I met four people this morning, the poker face, the baby stare, the icy mitt, and the peace that passeth understanding—let the place be dedicated to X, the unknown factor, to the Missing Link, to Jo Jo the dog-faced boy, to the Sargossa Sea, to Humpty Dumpty, to Little Red Riding Hood crying for her mother, to those who never believe in Santa Klaus, to the man who turned himself inside out because he was so sleepy.

9

Steps on steps lift on into the sky; the lengths count up into stairways; let me go up for the Redeemer is up there; He died for me; so a Spanish Indian was speaking—and he asked, When the first French Jesuit looked from Yavapai four hundred years ago, did he murmur of a tall altar to go on a mile-long rock shelf down there on a mesa? did he whisper of an unspeakably tall altar there for the raising of the ostensorium and the swinging of censers and the calling up of the presence of the Heart of the Living Christ? And he went on, Where the Son of God is made known surely is a place for the removal of shoes and the renewal of feet for the journey—surely this is so.

10

Came a lean, hungry-looking hombre with Kansas, Nebraska, the Dakotas on his wind-bitten face, and he was saying, Sure my boy, sure my girl, and you're free to have any sweet bluebird fancies you please, any wild broncho thoughts you choose to have, when you stand before this grand scrap-pile of hats, hammers, haciendas, and hidalgos. He went on, Yes, let this be dedicated to Time and Ice; a memorial of the Human Family which came, was, and went; let it stand as a witness of the short miserable pilgrimage of mankind, of flame faiths, of blood and fire, and of Ice which was here first and will be here again—Faces once frozen you shall all be frozen again—the little clocks of Man shall all be frozen and nobody will be too late or too early ever again.

11

On the rim a quizzical gray-glinting hombre was telling himself how
it looked to him—the sun and the air are endless with silver tricks—
the light of the sun has crimson stratagems—the changes go in stop-
watch split seconds—the blues slide down a box of yellow and mix
with reds that melt into gray and come back saffron clay and granite
pink—a weaving gamble of color twists on and it is anybody's guess
what is next.

A long sand-brown shawl shortens to a glimmering turquoise scarf—
as the parapets and chimneys wash over and out in the baths of the
sunset and the floats of the gloaming, one man says, There goes God
with an army of banners, and another man, Who is God and why?
who am I and why?

> He told himself, This may be
> something else than what I
> see when I look—how do I
> know? For each man sees him-
> self in the Grand Canyon—
> each one makes his own Canyon
> before he comes, each one brings
> and carries away his own Canyon—
> who knows? and how do I know?

12

> If the wind has a song, it
> is moaning: Good Lawd, I
> done done what you told me
> to do.

> When the scrapers of the
> deep winds were done, and
> the haulers of the tall
> waters had finished, this
> was the accomplishment.

> The moon goes down here
> as a dark bellringer doing

once more what he has done
over and over already in
his young life.

Up on a long blue platform
comes a line of starprints.

The drums of the sun never
get tired, and first off
every morning, the drums of
the sun perform an intro-
duction of the dawn here.

Thomas Wolfe

GULPING THE GREAT WEST

*W*olfe's *literary reputation rests on the exhilarated celebration of America that forms his four prodigious novels. Yet he was aware that his books were anything but representative of the entire country. In 1935, when he had occasion to make a quick stopover at the Grand Canyon, the sight made him mindful of what he had been missing. "I begin to see how inadequate all I have said and written about this country really is," he confided to his editor, Maxwell Perkins. So in late June of 1938, when he got a spur-of-the-moment invitation to "do" the finest scenery in the West, there was no hesitating. Wolfe saw this "Great Parks Trip" as a chance to fill a large gap in his experience.*

The novelist's company was Edward M. Miller, an editor with the Portland Oregonian, *and Ray Conway, an official of the Oregon State Motor Association. Their plan: ten national parks and 4632 road miles in thirteen days. Wolfe didn't set the itinerary, but its scale was completely in character.*

Wolfe intended to work up his diary of the trip into permanent form, but he never even had the chance to have it transcribed from its gray clothbound ledger, the kind in which he habitually wrote out first drafts of his work. Not a week after his parks trip ended, Wolfe contracted pneumonia or influenza on a cruise ship. It marked the start of a rapid dissolution of his health, and on September 15 he died. His fragmentary observations of the "Great Parks Trip" can only suggest the power of the book which would have been. The diary, finally published in 1951, turned out to be the last manuscript Wolfe ever wrote. It is best read forgetting it is unfinished, for its clipped cadences, suggestive of free verse, stand as the finest poetry ever written about the national parks.

JUNE 20: TO CRATER LAKE

LEFT PORTLAND, University Club, 8:15 sharp—Fair day, bright sunlight, no cloud in sky—Went South by East through farmlands of upper Willamette and around base of Mount Hood which was glowing in brilliant sun—Then climbed and crossed Cascades, and came down with suddenness of knife into the dry lands of the Eastern slope—Then over high plateau and through bare hills and canyons and irrigated farmlands here and there, low valley, etc., and into Bent at 12:45—200 miles in 4½ hours—

Then lunch at hotel and view of the 3 Sisters and the Cascade range—then up to the Pilot Butte above the town—the great plain stretching infinite away—and unapproachable the great line of the Cascades with their snowspiraled sentinels Hood, Adams, Jefferson, 3 Sisters, etc, and out of Bend at 3 and then through the vast and level pinelands—somewhat reminiscent of the South for 100 miles then down through the noble pines to the vast plainlike valley of the Klamath?—the virgin land of Canaan all again—the far-off ranges—infinite—Oregon and the Promised Land—then through the valley floor—past Indian reservation—Capt Jack—the Modocs—the great trees open approaching vicinity of the Park—the entrance and the reservation—the forester—the houses—the great snow patches underneath the trees—then the great climb upwards—the foresting, administration—up and up again—through the passes the great plain behind and at length the incredible crater of the lake—the hotel and a certain cheerlessness in spite of cordialness—dry tongues vain-licking for a feast—the return, the cottages, the college boys and girls who serve and wait—the cafeteria and the souvenirs—the great crater fading coldly in incredible cold light—at

length departure—and the forest rangers down below—long, long talks—too long with them about "our wonders", etc—then by dark-

ness the sixty or seventy miles down the great dim expanse of Klamath Lake, the decision to stay here for the night—3 beers, a shower, and this, reveille at 5:30 in the morning—and so to bed!

First day: 404 miles

The gigantic unconscious humor of the situation—C "making every national park" without seeing any of them—the main thing is to "make them"—and so on and on tomorrow. . . .

EVENING, JUNE 21: INTO YOSEMITE

. . . the San Joaquin Valley now—and bursting with Gods plenty—orchards—peaches—apricots—and vineyards—orange groves—Gods plenty of the best—and glaring little towns sown thick with fruit packing houses—ovenhot, glittering in the hot and shining air—town after town—each in the middle of Gods plenty—and at length the turn at —————— toward Yosemite—90 miles away—and a few miles from town the hills again—the barren, crateric, lavic, volcanic blasted hills—but signs now telling us we can't get in now across the washed out road save behind the conductor—and now too late—already 5 of six and the last conductor leaves

at six and we still 50 miles away—and telephone calls now to rangers, superintendents and so forth, a filling station and hot cabins, and the end of a day of blazing heat and the wind stirring in the sycamores

about the cabins, and on again now, and almost immediately the broken
ground, the straw light mouldings, the rises to the crater hills and soon
    among them—climbing, climbing into timber—and down down
down into pleasant timbered mountain folds—get no sensation yet
and winding in and out—and little hill towns here and there and climbing, climbing, climbing, mountain lodges, cabins, houses, and so on,
and now in terrific mountain folds, close packed, precipitous, lapped
together and down and over, down again
    along breath taking curves and steepnesses and sheer drops down
below into a canyon cut a mile below by great knifes blade—and at
the bottom the closed gate—the little store—calls upon the phone again,
and darkness and the sending notes, and at last success—upon our own
heads be the risk but we may enter—and we do—and so slowly up
    we go along the washed out road—finding it not near so dangerous
as we feared—and at length past the bad end and the closed gate and
release—and up now climbing and the sound of mighty waters in the
gorge and the sheer blacknesses of beetling masses and the stars—and
presently the entrance and the rangers house—a free pass now—and
up and up—and boles of trees terrific, cloven rock above the road
    and over us and dizzy masses night black as a cloud, a sense of the
imminent terrific and at length the valley of the Yosemite; roads forking
darkly, but the perfect sign—and now a smell of smokes and of gigantic
tentings and enormous trees and gigantic cliff walls night black all
around and above the sky-bowl of starred night—and Currys Lodge and
    smoky gaiety and wonder—hundreds of young faces and voices—
the offices, buildings stores, the dance floor crowded with its weary
hundreds and the hundreds of tents and cabins and the absurdity of
the life and the immensity of it all—and 1200 little shop girls and stenogs
and new-weds and schoolteachers and boys—all, God bless their
    little lives, necking, dancing, kissing, feeling, and embracing in the
great darkness of the giant redwood trees—all laughing and getting
loved tonight—and the sound of the dark gigantic fall of water—so
to bed!
And 535 miles today!

June 23: To the South Rim, Grand Canyon

    ... moving through timeless time and on and on across the
immense plain backed by more immensities of fiendish mountain

slopes to meet it and so almost meeting moveless-moving never meeting up and up and around and through a pass and down to Kingman and a halt for water and on and on and up and down into another mighty plain, desert growing grey-green greener—and some cattle now and always up and up and through fried blasted slopes and the enormous

lemon-magic of the desert plains, fiend mountain slopes pure lemon heat mist as from magic seas arising—and a halt for gas at a filling station with a water fountain "Please be careful with the water we have to haul it 60 miles"—5280 feet above—and 4800 feet we've climbed since Needles and on and on and up and the country greening now and

steers in fields wrenching grey-green among sage brush clumps and trees beginning now—the National Forest beginning—and new greenery—and trees and pines and grass again—a world of desert greenness still not Oregon—but a different world entirely from the desert world and hill slopes no longer fiend troubled but now friendly, forested familiar, and around and

down and in a pleasant valley Williams—and for a beer here where I *thought* I was 3 years ago—bartender a Mexican or an Indian or both and out and on our way again only the great road leading across the continent and 6 or 7 miles out an off turn to the left for the Grand Canyon—and not much climbing now, but up and down again the great plateau 7000 feet

on top—and green fields now and grass and steers and hills forested and cooler and trees and on and on toward (levelly) the distant twin rims—blue-vague defined—of the terrific canyon—the great sun sinking now below our 7000 feet—we racing on to catch him at the canyon ere he sinks entirely—but too late, too late—at last the rangers little house, the

permit and the sticker, the inevitable conversations, the polite goodbyes—and (almost dark now) at 8:35 to the edges of the canyon—to Bright Angel Lodge—and before we enter between the cabins of the Big Gorgooby—and the Big Gorgooby there immensely, darkly, almost weirdly there—a fathomless darkness peered at from the very edge of hell with abysmal starlight—almost unseen—just

fathomlessly there—So to our cabin—and delightful service—and so to dinner in the Lodge—and our rudeeleven in jodphurs, pajamas, shirts, and country suits, and Fred Harvey's ornate wigwam—and to dinner here—and then to walk along the rim of Big Gorgooby and inspect the big hotel—and at the stars innumerable and immense above the Big Gorgooby just a look—a big look—so goodnight and 500 miles today—

June 24: South Rim to North Rim

At daybreak a deer outside the window cropping grass.

Rose Grand Canyon 8:15—others had been up already for an hour—wakened at four or thereabouts by deer grazing, and by its hard small feet outside of window—Then Miller in at 8:30—but let me sleep—so bathed, dressed, to coffee shop by G and good breakfast then packed with Miller Conway and the Ranger to Administration offices, met the Ass't Super.—so to Observation point—the Ranger along and looked through observation at

Old Gorgooby and unvital time—and Alberdene the young geologist with crisp-curly hair and cheery personality who talked and remembered me from 3 yr. ago—an Arizona PhD and at Harvard too—but now wants no more teaching and applies for Philippines—so down to Lookout Tower where the young caravan streams in and listens to lecture by young Ranger Columbia and into tower and all the people—the Eastern cowboy with Fred Harvey hat and

shirt and cowgirl with broad hat, and wet red mouth, blonde locks and riding breeches filled with buttock—and up into tower and the Painted Desert and the Small Gorgooby gorge—and the Vermillion Cliffs—and down and goodbye to the ranger—and so away—and stop over for a look at Small Gorgooby gorge—and on to the desert and to Cameron and blazing

heat and the demented reds again and lunch here in an Indian Lodgeee —and an old dog moving in the shadow of a wall—and so away across the bridge and into the Painted Desert and blazing heat and baked road and Painted Desert through the afternoon by the Vermillion Cliffs—and four small Indian girls in rags and petticoats beside the road awaiting pennies (dimes they got) two upon a burro—beer, and photographs and heat incredible and the demented reds of Painted Desert and away away again good road—bad road—good and bad again by the demented and fiend tortured redness of Vermillion Cliffs—red, mauve, and violet, passing into red again—and now the gorge, much smaller down, of Big

Gorgooby, and the Navajo Bridge—and the Gorgooby, brown-red-yellow—a mere 1000 feet or so below—and on and on across the Big

Gorgooby now through desert land—now grey-greening sagely into
sage and stray Indians moving into road here and there and Indian
houses—then the far lift of the rise, the road rising, winding into hills,
and up and up into

the timber and the forest now, and all the lovely quaking aspens
and the vast and rising rim of sage and meadow land—a golf course
big and narrow on both sides—rising clearly and mysteriously to
woods—and then the big woods again, and deep dense woods, the
rangers house and entrance, and at last the Lodge, the mysterious
colour, a haircut, a clean shirt and supper with the Browns, and a sweet
waitress, and before this past—the sunset moment—the tremendous
twilight of the Big Gorgooby—more concise and more collected, more
tremendous here—and dimmer then and darkness and the lights of
the South Rim—and later on the moving picture the two Canadian
College quartettes in crimson blazers—the inevitable theatrical
performance with the

waitresses and bellhops performing—Hiawatha chanting the U. P.—
and naught but the clog dancers passable—and then Brown and his
colored picture slides—Bryce, Zion, the Canyon, and the Mormon
temple, then the dance, the bar, Scotch highballs, and good talk with
Miller, and the wind in the pine trees, and leave with Miller to the
cabin, and

C. still wakeful, rising, reading costs and mileages excitably from
his records—he all the night with them—and arguments, agreements,
and accounts again on costs and mileages and possibilities—the moon
in 30 hrs. is possible—and C taking pride in all our present luxury
because "It makes a better person of you" and the first time he gave a
man a tip—and so to bed! And 210 miles today

June 25: North Rim and Zion

Rose 7:30 North Rim Lodge Grand Canyon—shave, bath, dressed—
Cabin very luxurious—appointed like modern hotel—best we'd seen—
Sound of waitresses and maids singing farewell songs—"Till we meet
again" etc—to passengers departing on buses—Traveling U. P. sentiment and C declared there were tears in eyes of passengers and some
of the girls—Into Lodge for view from terrace of the Big Gorgooby
in first light—and glorious—! and glorious!—wrote half dozen post cards
in brilliant sunlight as before—then into breakfast with C and M and

the Browns—and the inevitable Ranger—and the waitress with the strange and charming smile—and she from Texas and admitted that sentiment, songs, and kicking her legs for Pony Boy in night time entertainment all at 8000 feet for dear old U. P. got her wind and at first "made her awfully tired"—So out and by myself again to terrace—then to cabin to pack—then to hotel—and with Ranger and C and M to cafeteria for the inevitable inspection of cabins, cafeterias, etc—and at long last, at 11 o'clock

on our way out—and down through the Forest, and the long sweeping upland meadows and the deer and cattle grazing, quivering the aspen leaves in the bright air, and down and down and then the bottomlands spread below us over again, the fierce red earth, the tortured buttes and the Vermillion Cliffs, the Painted desert, and on and on across the desert and into Utah, and at 1:30, 3 miles past the

line, the Mormon town of Kanab at Perry's Lodge—a white house, pleasant and almost New England, and the fiery bright heat, the little town, and greenness here, and trees and grass, and a gigantic lovely cool-bright poplar at the corner—and so out and on along the road and presently the turn off to the left for Zion's Canyon—and before the mountains rising range and range, no longer

fierce red and vermillion now, but sandy, whitest limestones, striped with strange stripes of salmon pink—scrub dotted, paler—Now in the canyon road and climbing, and now pink rock again, strange shapes and scarings in the rock, and even vertices upon huge swathes of stone, and plunging down now in stiff canyon folds the sheer solid beetling

soaplike block of salmon red again—deeper yet not so fierce and strange (as I thought) as the Grand Canyon earth, and towering soapstone blocks of red incredible, and through a tunnel, out and down and down, and through the great one spaced with even windows in the rock that give on magic casements opening on sheer blocks of soapstone red, and out again

in the fierce light and down round dizzying windings of the road into the canyons depth and at the bottom halt inevitable at Administration Offices, visit inevitable to cafeteria and cabins, and away again along the canyon and the Virgin River (how sweet to see sweet water flowing here between these dizzy soapstone blocks of red) and round

the bendings of the river by the soapstone walls of blank fierce red and into the valley floor and trees (a little like Yosemite, this valley, yet not so lush, so cool, nor so enchanted, nor cooled by the dun-

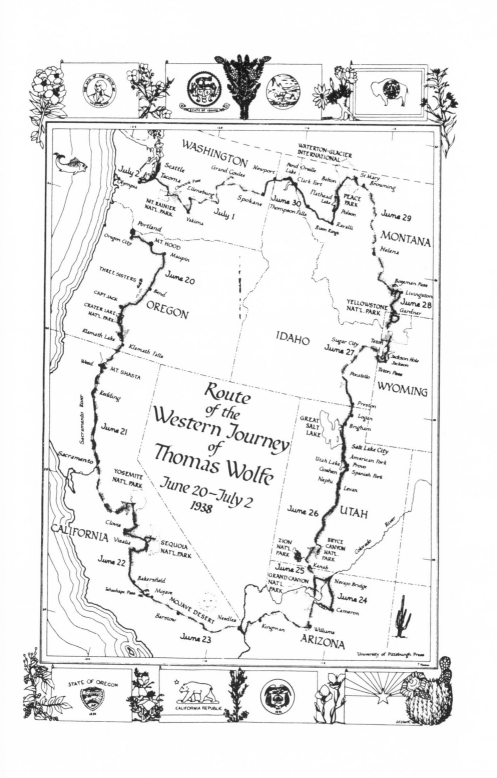

Route
of the
Western Journey
of
Thomas Wolfe
June 20–July 2
1938

University of Pittsburgh Press

blanket of towering pines, but an oasis here, a glimpse of lodge inevitable and—O miracle!—in hot oasis a swimming pool, a bathing house,
and young wet half-naked forms—a pool surrounded

by the cottonwoods and walled around, beetled over by sheer soapstone blocks of red capped by pinnacles of blazing white—O pool in
cottonwoods surrounded by fierce blocks of red and temples and kings
thrones and the sheer smoothness of the bloody vertices of soapstone
red—did never pool look cooler, nor water wetter, wetter more
inviting. . . .

June 25 and 26: Bryce Canyon

. . . and so away, and a shot at a white lime-cliff on the way, and
up and up again, and through the tunnel, and by the

strange carved slopes and vertical and punctual lines, and to the top
and down and down again a vista of plain and desert, and the white
sand-lime peaks with salmon markings—and one strange, isolate and
Painted Desertward (I think) of salmon red and down and down and
to the main road finally and to the left and up along it toward Bryce's
Canyon on the main

road north to Salt Lake City—and now, almost immediate, a greener
land, and grass in semi-desert fields, and stock and cattle grazing, and
now timbered hills in contour not unlike the fields of home, and now
farms and green incredible of fields and hay and mowing and things
growing and green trees and Canaan pleasantness and a river flowing
(the Sevier) and (by desert comparison) a fruitful valley—and occasional little towns—small Mormon towns—sometimes with little houses
of old brick—but mostly little houses of frame, and for the most part
mean and plain and stunted looking and hills rising to the left—a vista
of salmon pink, Vermillion Cliffs again—the barricades of Bryce—and

then the turn in—and so halted here by road repair until the convoy
from the Canyon passes out—and meanwhile talking to the man with
the red flag—"we have no deserts here in Utah"—is Zion then a flower-
ing prairie, and are Salt Lake and the Bonneville Flats the grassy precincts of the King's Paradise—and cars gathered here on bleeding oil—

from Ohio—New Mexico—Illinois—California—Michigan—and
presently the other cavalcade appears upon the crest and flash down-
wards one by one till all are through—and then we start—the road
good but still oil-bloody to the right for seven or ten miles—and up

through sage land into timber, past corrals, dude ranches etc, into
timber on the high plateau, another Rangers entrance house in view,
the stick-candy-whipping of the flag—another sticker—seven now—
and into the park and up and through the timber past the Lodge and
to the river, where stand in setting sun looking out and down upon
the least overwhelming, dizzy, and least massive of the lot—but perhaps
the most astounding—a million wind-blown pinnacles of salmon pink
and fiery white all fused together like stick candy—all suggestive of
a childs fantasy of heaven and beyond the open semi-green and semi-
desert plain—and lime-white and scrub dotted mountains—and so back
and to the Lodge with sour-pussed oldsters on the veranda, trinkets
souvenirs, and, methought, some superciliousness within, so we got
our keys, and to our cabin, and so shaved, and to the cafeteria which
was clean and much be-Indian-souvenired betrinketed, somehow
depressing, and expensive—pie ten 15 cents and 20 for a bad and messy
sandwich—and so to the Lodge and peeked in at the inevitable Ranger
and the attentive
dutiful sourpusses listening to the inevitable lecture—Flora and Fauna
of Bryce Canyon—so bought post cards and wrote them—and so to
my cabin to write this.
And after this to Lodge where dinner going on, and into curio shop
where, with some difficulty bought beer in cans, and had two, feeling
more and more desolate in this most unreal state of Utah, and
struck up talk with quaint old blondined wag named Florence who
imitates bird calls and dark rather attractive woman, Canadian probably French, who sold curios and who had life in her—and was
obviously willing to share it—So talking with them in lobby until
dinner broke up at 10:30 and young people coming out looking rather
lost and vaguely eager, I thought, as if they wanted something that
wasn't there and didn't know how
to find it—and had some depressing reflections on Americans in
search of gaiety, and National Park Lodges, and Utah and frustration,
etc; so home, where found C busy with his calculations—"if we do
so and so tomorrow, we'll have only so and so much to do on
Monday"—and wrote this, my companions sleeping—and so to bed!
About 265 miles today!

Arose Bryce Canyon 7:30 dressed, walked with M to Rim and to
observation house on point and looked at Canyon. Sky somewhat

overcast and no sunlight in the canyon, but it was no less amazing—
looked fragile compared to other great canyons "like filigree work",
of fantastic loveliness Great shouldering bulwarks of eroded sand going
down to it—made it look very brittle and soft— erodes at rate of 1
inch a year—something the effect of sugar candy at a carnival—
powdery—whitey—melting away—Old man, roughly dressed, and with
one tooth, and wife, and daughter, surprisingly smart looking young
female in pajama slacks and smoked goggles talking geology—

the words came trippingly off her tongue—"erosion"—"wind
erosion"—"125 million years and so on"—There had been argument with
someone whether Canyon had been cut with water—"all canyons cut
with water" etc—M took pictures "Look out as if you're looking out"—
then quickly back through woods toward lodge and after last nights
rain brightly amazingly pungent, sweet and fragrant—smell of sage,
pine needles, etc—So breakfast in lodge and C as usual engrossed with
hotel manager haggling about prices, rates, cabin accommodations
etc—wrote

post cards and ate hearty breakfast and talked with waitress who
was from Purdue—studying "home economics" and dress designing
and hopes to be a "buyer" for Chicago store—observed the tourists—
two grim featured females—school-teachers—at table next—who
glowered dourly at everyone and everything with stiff inflexible faces
and H. says most of the tourists are women and many school teachers
—So the tourists rose to depart, and presently the sound of singing
and the waitresses, maids, bell boys etc gathered in front of the Lodge
and by bus singing "Till we meet again"—"Good-bye, ladies" etc—and
one of the dour looking school teachers dabbing furtively at eyes, and
the bus departing, and emotional farewells, and the young folks departing back to their work, and bragging exultantly "We got tears out of
four of 'em this morning. Oh, I love to see 'em cry; it means business"—
Then discussing hotel business again and the art of pleasing guests and
squeezing tears from them—and for me the memory of

the dour faced teacher dabbing at her eyes and stabbing pity in the
heart and something that can not be said. . . .

III

PREMONITIONS AND ADMONITIONS

ENCOUNTERS WITH THINGS TO COME

IN THIS final section, the readings all communicate the future, though in different ways. The prescient quality of George Catlin's vision, uncanny in retrospect, was more the result of a painterly flight of fancy than a reasoned working-out of the national park idea; for that, we have Frederick Law Olmsted to thank. Paternalistic as it was, the Lowell industrial plan, described here by Charles Dickens, heralded some of the advances which blue-collar women have only recently begun to make in the American workplace. The essays by Bayard Taylor and Mark Twain, who were ostensibly writing in description of striking geological features, are really mood-pieces that catch an otherworldliness in which all modes of time—past, present, and future—merge.

Much of this anthology has imputed a timelessness to the national parks. We have had them for well over a century now; as they have aged, they have acquired a beguiling bouquet of inevitability. Yet if it is true, as it seems to be, that humankind's capacity for spoliation grows a little bigger each day, then is the continued existence of the parks to be taken for granted?

There is a lot of talk, in connection with the national parks, about "future generations." Some of this is vacant breath, boilerplate, the clattering of bureaucrats. Some, though, is spoken in earnest, and those who speak it are necessarily candid about the unsecured—the never-to-be-secured—future of the parks. The pieces by James Bryce and Wallace Stegner are marked by this candor, and prefigure the admonitory themes which have dominated national park writing since the 1960s.

George Catlin

A NATION'S PARK

Catlin was first and foremost a painter, whose fame, rightfully, rests on his portraits of American Indian life. He also played the journalist, however, and recorded for Eastern readers the details of his Western travels. It was in one of these letters, published in 1833 in the New York Daily Commercial Advertiser, that he voiced the need for "some great protecting policy of government" to secure "a nation's Park" to protect both the lifeways of the Indians and the native game upon which they depended. If only white settlers would leave off slaughtering the buffalo, and if "a system of non-intercourse" could be established instead, then the communities of the Indians might be perpetuated.

These brief remarks have since brought Catlin wide recognition as the first person to envision the concept of a national park. Essentially this is correct, though it should be remembered that William Wordsworth was calling for a "national property" in England's Lake District at about this time. Moreover, several foreign observers of the United States, among them Alexis de Tocqueville, were even then warning American readers that they would be sorry if they allowed their country to be despoiled.

Putting aside the question of precedence, Catlin's statement deserves its fame, if for nothing else than its forcefulness. Nevertheless, though his *reasoning was echoed by Emerson and others, there is no evidence that these scattered strands of thought had any influence on the Yosemite-Mariposa land grant of 1864—the true beginning of the national park movement in the United States.*

MANY ARE the rudenesses and wilds in Nature's works, which are destined to fall before the deadly axe and desolating hands of cultivating man; and so amongst her ranks of *living*, of beast and human, we often find noble stamps, or beautiful colours, to which our admiration clings; and even in the overwhelming march of civilized improvements and refinements do we love to cherish their existence, and lend our efforts to preserve them in their primitive rudeness. Such of Nature's works are always worthy of our preservation and protection; and the further we become separated (and the face of the country) from that pristine wildness and beauty the more pleasure does the mind of enlightened man feel in recurring to those scenes, when he can have them preserved for his eyes and his mind to dwell upon.

Of such "rudenesses and wilds," Nature has no where presented more beautiful and lovely scenes, than those of the vast prairies of the West; and of *man* and *beast,* no nobler specimens than those who inhabit them—the *Indian* and the *buffalo*—joint and original tenants of the soil, and fugitives together from the approach of civilized man; they have fled to the great plains of the West, and there, under an equal doom, they have taken up their *last abode,* where their race will expire, and their bones will bleach together.

It may be that *power* is *right,* and *voracity* a *virtue;* and that these people, and these noble animals, are *righteously* doomed to an issue that *will* not be averted.

It can be easily proved—we have a civilized science that can easily do it, or anything else that may be required to cover the iniquities of civilized man in catering for his unholy appetites. It can be proved that the weak and ignorant have no *rights*—that there can be no virtue in darkness—that God's gifts have no meaning or merit until they are appropriated by civilized man—by him brought into the light, and converted to his use and luxury. We have a mode of reasoning (I forget what it is called) by which all this can be proved, and even more. The *word* and the *system* are entirely of *civilized* origin; and latitude is admirably given to them in proportion to the increase of civilized wants, which often require a *judge* to overrule the laws of nature. I say that *we* can prove such things; but an *Indian* cannot. It is a mode of reasoning unknown to him in his nature's simplicity, but admirably adapted to subserve the interests of the enlightened world, who are always their own judges, when dealing with the savage; and who, in the present refined age, have many appetites that can only be lawfully indulged, by proving God's laws defective.

It is not enough in this polished and extravagant age, that we get from the Indian his lands, and the very clothes from his back, but the food from their mouths must be stopped, to add a new and useless article to the fashionable world's luxuries. The ranks must be thinned, and the race exterminated, of this noble animal, and the Indians of the great plains left without the means of supporting life, that white men may figure a few years longer, enveloped in buffalo robes—that they may spread them, for their pleasure and elegance, over the backs of their sleighs, and trail them ostentatiously amidst the busy throng, as things of beauty and elegance that have been made for them!

Reader! listen to the following calculations, and forget them not. The buffaloes (the quadrupeds from whose backs your beautiful robes were taken, and whose myriads were once spread over the whole country, from the Rocky Mountains to the Atlantic Ocean) have recently fled before the appalling appearance of civilized man, and taken up their abode and pasturage amid the almost boundless prairies of the West. An instinctive dread of their deadly foes, who made an easy prey of them whilst grazing in the forest, has led them to seek the midst of the vast and treeless plains of grass, as the spot where they would be least exposed to the assaults of their enemies; and it is exclusively in those desolate fields of silence (yet of beauty) that they are to be found—and over these vast steppes, or prairies, have they fled, like the Indian, toward the "setting sun"; until their bands have been crowded together, and their limits confined to a narrow strip of country on this side of the Rocky Mountains. This strip of country, which extends from the province of Mexico to lake Winnipeg on the North, is almost one entire plain of grass, which is, and ever must be, useless to cultivating man. It is here, and here chiefly, that the buffaloes dwell; and with, and hovering about them, live and flourish the tribes of Indians, whom God made for the enjoyment of that fair land and its luxuries.

It is a melancholy contemplation for one who has travelled as I have, through these realms, and seen this noble animal in all its pride and glory, to contemplate it so rapidly wasting from the world, drawing the irresistible conclusion too, which one must do, that its species is soon to be extinguished, and with it the peace and happiness (if not the actual existence) of the tribes of Indians who are joint tenants with them, in the occupancy of these vast and idle plains. And what a splendid contemplation too, when one (who has travelled these realms, and can duly appreciate them) imagines them as they *might* in future be seen, (by some great protecting policy of government) preserved in their pristine beauty and wildness, in a *magnificent park*, where the world could see for ages to come, the native Indian in his classic attire, galloping his wild horse, with sinewy bow, and shield and lance, amid the fleeting herds of elks and buffaloes. What a beautiful and thrilling specimen for America to preserve and hold up to the view of her refined citizens and the world, in future ages! A *nation's Park*, containing man and beast, in all the wild and freshness of their nature's beauty!

I would ask no other monument to my memory, nor any other enrolment of my name amongst the famous dead, than the reputation of having been the founder of such an institution.

Such scenes might easily have been preserved, and still could be cherished on the great plains of the West, without detriment to the country or its borders; for the tracts of country on which the buffaloes have assembled, are uniformly sterile, and of no available use to cultivating man. It is on these plains, which are stocked with buffaloes, that the finest specimens of the Indian race are to be seen. It is here, that the savage is decorated in his richest costume. It is here, and here only, that his wants are all satisfied, and even the *luxuries* of life are afforded him in abundance. And here also is he the proud and honourable man (before he has had teachers or laws), above the imported wants, which beget meanness and vice; stimulated by ideas of honour and virtue, in which the God of Nature has certainly not curtailed him.

There are, by a fair calculation, more than 300,000 Indians, who are now subsisted on the flesh of the buffaloes, and by those animals supplied with all the luxuries of life which they desire, as they know of none others. The great variety of uses to which they convert the body and other parts of the animal, are almost incredible to the person who has not actually dwelt amongst these people, and closely studied their modes and customs. Every part of their flesh is converted to food, in one shape or another, and on it they barely subsist. The robes of the animals are worn by the Indians instead of blankets—their skins are tanned, are used as coverings for their lodges, and for their beds; undressed, they are used for constructing canoes—for saddles, for bridles—l'arrêts, lassos, and thongs. The horns are shaped into ladles and spoons—the brains are used for dressing the skins—their bones are used for saddle trees—for war clubs, and scrapers for graining the robes—and others are broken up for the marrow-fat which is contained in them. Their sinews are used for strings and backs to their bows—for thread to string their beads and sew their dresses. The feet of the animals are boiled, with their hoofs, for the glue they contain, for fastening their arrow points, and many other uses. The hair from the head and shoulders, which is long, is twisted and braided into halters, and the tail is used for a fly-brush. In this wise do these people convert and use the various parts of this useful animal, and with all these luxuries of life about them, and their numerous games, they are happy (God bless them) in the ignorance of the disastrous fate that awaits them.

Yet this interesting community, with its sports, its wildnesses, its languages, and all its manners and customs, could be perpetuated, and also the buffaloes, whose numbers would increase and supply them with food for ages and centuries to come, if a system of non-intercourse could be established and preserved. But such is not to be the case—the buffalo's doom is sealed, and with their extinction must assuredly sink into real despair and starvation, the inhabitants of these vast plains, which afford for the Indians, no other possible means of subsistence; and they must at last fall a prey to wolves and buzzards, who will have no other bones to pick.

Reader, I will stop here, lest you might forget to answer these important queries—these are questions which I know will puzzle the world—and, perhaps, it is not right that I should ask them.

Frederick Law Olmsted

PRESERVATION FOR ALL

On June 30, 1864, some seven months after making his speech at Gettysburg, President Lincoln signed an order which proved to be the start of the American national parks movement. He approved an act to withdraw the Yosemite Valley and the nearby Mariposa Grove of sequoias from the public domain and give them to the state of California—on the condition that they be held "inalienable for all time" for the "use, resort and recreation" of the public. While the Yosemite-Mariposa grant didn't create a national park (Yellowstone was the first, in 1872), it marked the first time Congress had reserved federal land for a nonutilitarian purpose.

California accepted the grant. The governor then appointed a commission to make recommendations for overseeing it. At the head of the commission was Frederick Law Olmsted, the country's foremost landscape architect. As the designer (with Calvert Vaux) and first superintendent of New York City's Central Park, Olmsted was better qualified than anyone else for the unprecedented task of writing a plan for a park expressly devoted to preserving a natural area for the benefit of the entire country. In August 1865 Olmsted presented his report for the first time, before his fellow commissioners.

For reasons still not fully known, the California legislature never saw the report; it apparently was squelched by someone on the commission.

In any event, the manuscript disappeared, almost without a trace. A copy was finally found in Olmsted's office in 1952.

The State of California managed the Yosemite-Mariposa grant so poorly that in 1889 John Muir and Robert Underwood Johnson (the editor of Century, then the nation's most influential magazine) began a sixteen-year campaign to create Yosemite National Park. Had Olmsted's report been made known, it undoubtedly would have become a philosophical source for Muir and Johnson and the rest of the first generation of national park advocates. No other writer of the day understood as well as Olmsted that the beneficial effects of unadulterated natural beauty can and should be enjoyed by all classes of people, not just the cultured rich. Equally far-seeing, in light of current problems facing the parks, were his concerns about visitor pressures and invading exotic plant species.

As it turned out, Olmsted's fate, in connection with the national parks movement, was to be something of a prophet without honor. Ironically, his home in Brookline, Massachusetts, is now a National Historic Site.

THE MAIN feature of the Yo Semite is best indicated in one word as a chasm. It is a chasm nearly a mile in average width, however, and more than ten miles in length. The central and broader part of this chasm is occupied at the bottom by a series of groves of magnificent trees, and meadows of the most varied, luxuriant and exquisite herbage, through which meanders a broad stream of the clearest water, rippling over a pebbly bottom and eddying among banks of ferns and rushes; sometimes narrowed into sparkling rapids and sometimes expanding into placid pools which reflect the wondrous heights on either side. The walls of the chasm are generally half a mile, sometimes nearly a mile in height above these meadows, and where most lofty are nearly perpendicular, sometimes overjutting. At frequent intervals, however, they are cleft, broken, terraced and sloped, and in these places, as well as everywhere upon the summit, they are overgrown by thick clusters of trees.

There is nothing strange or exotic in the character of the vegetation; most of the trees and plants, especially those of the meadows and the waterside, are closely allied to and are not readily distinguished from those most common in the landscapes of the Eastern States or the midland counties of England. The stream is such a one as Shakespeare

Nevada Fall

delighted in, and brings pleasing reminiscences to the traveller of the Avon or the upper Thames.

Banks of heartsease and beds of cowslips and daisies are frequent, and thickets of dogwood, alder and willow often fringe the shores. At several points streams of water flow into the chasm, descending at one leap from five hundred to fourteen hundred feet. One small stream falls, in three closely consecutive pitches, a distance of two thousand six hundred feet, which is more than fifteen times the height of the falls of Niagara. In the spray of these falls superb rainbows are seen.

After midsummer a light, transparent haze generally pervades the atmosphere, giving an indescribable softness and exquisite dreamy charm to the scenery, like that produced by the Indian summer of the East. Clouds gathering at this season upon the snowy peaks which rise within forty miles on each side of the chasm to a height of over twelve thousand feet, sometimes roll down over the cliffs in the afternoon, and, under the influence of the rays of the setting sun, form the most gorgeous and magnificent thunderheads. The average elevation of the ground is higher than that of the highest peak of the White Mountains, or the Alleghenies, and the air is rare and bracing; yet, its temperature is never uncomfortably cool in summer, nor severe in winter.

The other district, associated with this by the act of Congress, consists of four sections of land, about thirty miles distant from it, on which stand in the midst of a forest composed of the usual trees and shrubs of the western slopes of the Sierra Nevada, about six hundred mature trees of the giant Sequoia. Among them is one known through numerous paintings and photographs as the Grizzly Giant, which probably is the noblest tree in the world. Besides this, there are hundreds of such beauty and stateliness that, to one who moves among them in the reverent mood to which they so strongly incite the mind, it will not seem strange that intelligent travellers have declared that they would rather have passed by Niagara itself than have missed visiting this grove.

By no statement of the elements of the scenery can any idea of that scenery be given, any more than a true impression can be conveyed of a human face by a measured account of its features. It is conceivable that any one or all of the cliffs of the Yo Semite might be changed in form and color, without lessening the enjoyment which is now obtained from the scenery. Nor is this enjoyment any more essentially derived from its meadows, its trees, its streams; least of all can it be attributed to the cascades. These, indeed, are scarcely to be named among the elements of the scenery. They are mere incidents, of far less consequence any day of the summer than the imperceptible humidity of the atmosphere and the soil. The chasm remains when they are dry, and the scenery may be, and often is, more effective, by reason of some temporary condition of the air, of clouds, of moonlight, or of sunlight through mist or smoke, in the season when the cascades attract the least attention, than when their volume of water is largest and their roar like constant thunder.

There are falls of water elsewhere finer, there are more stupendous rocks, more beetling cliffs, there are deeper and more awful chasms, there may be as beautiful streams, as lovely meadows, there are larger trees. It is in no scene or scenes the charm consists, but in the miles of scenery where cliffs of awful height and rocks of vast magnitude and of varied and exquisite coloring, are banked and fringed and draped and shadowed by the tender foliage of noble and lovely trees and bushes, reflected from the most placid pools, and associated with the most tranquil meadows, the most playful streams, and every variety of soft and peaceful pastoral beauty.

The union of the deepest sublimity with the deepest beauty of nature, not in one feature or another, not in one part or one scene or another, not in any landscape that can be framed by itself, but all around and wherever the visitor goes, constitutes the Yo Semite the greatest glory of nature. No photograph or series of photographs, no paintings ever prepare a visitor so that he is not taken by surprise, for could the scenes be faithfully represented the visitor is affected not only by that upon which his eye is at any moment fixed, but by all that with which on every side it is associated, and of which it is seen only as an inherent part. For the same reason no description, no measurements, no comparisons are of much value. Indeed the attention called by these to points in some definite way remarkable, by fixing the mind on mere matters of wonder or curiosity prevents the true and far more extraordinary character of the scenery from being appreciated.

It is the will of the nation as embodied in the act of Congress that this scenery shall never be private property, but that like certain defensive points upon our coast it shall be held solely for public purposes.

Two classes of considerations may be assumed to have influenced the action of Congress. The first and less important is the direct and obvious pecuniary advantage which comes to a commonwealth from the fact that it possesses objects which cannot be taken out of its domain, that are attractive to travellers and the enjoyment of which is open to all.

A more important class of considerations, however, remains to be stated. These are considerations of a political duty of grave importance to which seldom if ever before has proper respect been paid by any government in the world but the grounds of which rest on the same eternal base of equity and benevolence with all other duties of republican government. It is the main duty of government, if it is not the sole duty of government, to provide means of protection for all its citizens in the pursuit of happiness against all the obstacles, otherwise insurmountable, which the selfishness of individuals or combinations of individuals is liable to interpose to that pursuit.

It is a scientific fact that the occasional contemplation of natural scenes of an impressive character, particularly if this contemplation occurs in connection with relief from ordinary cares, change of air and change of habits, is favorable to the health and vigor of men and especially to the health and vigor of their intellect beyond any other conditions which can be offered them, that it not only gives pleasure for the time being but increases the subsequent capacity for happiness and the means of securing happiness. . . .

If we analyze the operation of scenes of beauty upon the mind, and consider the intimate relation of the mind upon the nervous system and the whole physical economy, the action and reaction which constantly occur between bodily and mental conditions, the reinvigoration which results from such scenes is readily comprehended. Few persons can see such scenery as that of the Yosemite and not be impressed by it in some slight degree. All not alike, all not perhaps consciously, and amongst all who are consciously impressed by it, few can give the least expression to that of which they are conscious. But there can be no doubt that all have this susceptibility, though with some it is much more dull and confused than with others.

The power of scenery to affect men is, in a large way, proportionate to the degree of their civilization and the degree in which their taste has been cultivated. Among a thousand savages there will be a much smaller number who will show the least sign of being so affected than among a thousand persons taken from a civilized community. This is only one of the many channels in which a similar distinction between civilized and savage men is to be generally observed. The whole body of the susceptibilities of civilized men and with their susceptibilities their powers, are on the whole enlarged.

But as with the bodily powers, if one group of muscles is developed by exercise exclusively, and all others neglected, the result is general feebleness, so it is with the mental faculties. And men who exercise those faculties or susceptibilities of the mind which are called in play by beautiful scenery so little that they seem to be inert with them, are either in a diseased condition from excessive devotion of the mind to a limited range of interests, or their whole minds are in a savage state; that is, in a state of low development. The latter class need to be drawn out generally; the former need relief from their habitual matters of interest and to be drawn out in those parts of their mental nature which have been habitually left idle and inert.

But there is a special reason why the reinvigoration of those parts which are stirred into conscious activity by natural scenery is more effective upon the general development and health than that of any other, which is this: The severe and excessive exercise of the mind which leads to the greatest fatigue and is the most wearing upon the whole constitution is almost entirely caused by application to the removal of something to be apprehended in the future, or to interests beyond those of the moment, or of the individual; to the laying up of wealth, to the preparation of something, to accomplishing something in the mind of another, and especially to small and petty details which are uninteresting in themselves and which engage the attention at all only because of the bearing they have on some general end of more importance which is seen ahead.

In the interest which natural scenery inspires there is the strongest contrast to this. It is for itself and at the moment it is enjoyed. The attention is aroused and the mind occupied without purpose, without a continuation of the common process of relating the present action, thought or perception to some future end. There is little else that has this quality so purely. . . .

Men who are rich enough and who are sufficiently free from anxiety with regard to their wealth can and do provide places of this needed recreation for themselves. They have done so from the earliest periods known in the history of the world, for the great men of the Babylonians, the Persians and the Hebrews, had their rural retreats, as large and luxurious as those of the aristocracy of Europe at present. There are in the islands of Great Britain and Ireland more than one thousand private parks and notable grounds devoted to luxury and recreation. The value of these grounds amounts to many millions of dollars and the cost of their annual maintenance is greater than that of the national schools; their only advantage to the commonwealth is obtained through the recreation they afford their owners (except as these extend hospitality to others) and these owners with their families number less than one in six thousand of the whole population. The enjoyment of the choicest natural scenes in the country and the means of recrea-

tion connected with them is thus a monopoly, in a very peculiar manner, of a very few, very rich people. The great mass of society, including those to whom it would be of the greatest benefit, is excluded from it. In the nature of the case private parks can never be used by the mass of the people in any country nor by any considerable number even of the rich, except by the favor of a few, and in dependence on them.

Thus without means are taken by government to withhold them from the grasp of individuals, all places favorable in scenery to the recreation of the mind and body will be closed against the great body of the people. For the same reason that the water of rivers should be guarded against private appropriation and the use of it for the purpose of navigation and otherwise protected against obstruction, portions of natural scenery may therefore properly be guarded and cared for by government. To simply reserve them from monopoly by individuals, however, it will be obvious, is not all that is necessary. It is necessary that they should be laid open to the use of the body of the people. The establishment by government of great public grounds for the free enjoyment of the people under certain circumstances, is thus justified and enforced as a political duty.

Such a provision, however, having regard to the whole people of a state, has never before been made and the reason it has not is evident.

It has always been the conviction of the governing classes of the old world that it is necessary that the large mass of all human communities should spend their lives in almost constant labor and that the power of enjoying beauty either of nature or of art in any high degree, requires a cultivation of certain faculties, which is impossible to these humble toilers. Hence it is thought better, so far as the recreations of the masses of a nation receive attention from their rulers, to provide artificial pleasure for them, such as theatres, parades, and promenades where they will be amused by the equipages of the rich and the animation of crowds.

It is unquestionably true that excessive and persistent devotion to sordid interests cramps and distorts the power of appreciating natural beauty and destroys the love of it which the Almighty has implanted in every human being, and which is so intimately and mysteriously associated with the moral perceptions and intuition, but it is not true that exemption from toil, much leisure, much study, much wealth, are necessary to the exercise of the esthetic and contemplative faculties. It is the folly of laws which have permitted and favored the monopoly by privileged classes of many of the means supplied in nature for the gratification, exercise and education of the esthetic faculties that has caused the appearance of dullness and weakness and disease of these faculties in the mass of the subjects of kings. And it is against the limitation of the means of such education to the rich that the wise legislation of free governments must be directed. . . .

It was in accordance with these views of the destiny of the New World and the duty of the republican government that Congress enacted that the Yosemite should be held, guarded and managed for the free use of the whole body of the people forever, and that the care of it, and the hospitality of admitting strangers from all parts of the world to visit it and enjoy it freely, should be a duty of dignity and be committed only to a sovereign state.

The trust having been accepted, it will be the duty of the legislature to define the responsibilities, the rights and powers of the Commissioners, whom by the Act of Congress, it will be the duty of the Executive of the state to appoint. These must be determined by a consideration of the purposes to which the ground is to be devoted and must be simply commensurate with those purposes.

The main duty with which the Commissioners should be charged should be to give every advantage practicable to the mass of people to benefit by that which is peculiar to this ground and which has caused Congress to treat it differently from other parts of the public domain. This peculiarity consists wholly in its natural scenery.

The first point to be kept in mind then is the preservation and maintenance as exactly as is possible of the natural scenery; the restriction, that is to say, within the narrowest limits consistent with the necessary accommodations of visitors, of all artificial constructions and the prevention of all constructions markedly inharmonious with the scenery or which would unnecessarily obscure, distort or detract from the dignity of the scenery.

In addition to the more immediate and obvious arrangements by which this duty is enforced there are two considerations which should not escape attention.

First: the value of the district in its present condition as a museum of natural science and the danger, indeed the certainty, that without care many of the species of plants now flourishing upon it will be lost and many interesting objects be defaced or obscured if not destroyed.

To illustrate these dangers, it may be stated that numbers of the native plants of large districts of the Atlantic states have almost wholly disappeared and that most of the common weeds of the farms are of foreign origin, having choked out the native vegetation. Many of the finer specimens of the most important trees in the scenery of the Yosemite have been already destroyed and the proclamation of the Governor, issued after the passage of the Act of Congress, forbidding the destruction of trees in the district, alone prevented the establishment of a saw mill within it. Notwithstanding the proclamation many fine trees have been felled and others girdled within a year. Indians and others have set fire to the forests and herbage and numbers of trees have been killed by these fires; the giant tree before referred to as probably the noblest tree now standing on the earth has been burned completely through the bark near the ground for a distance of more than one hundred feet of its circumference; not only have trees been cut, hacked, barked, and fired in prominent positions, but rocks in the midst of the most picturesque natural scenery have been broken, painted and discolored by fires built against them. In travelling to the Yosemite and within a few miles of the nearest point at which it can be approached by a wheeled vehicle, the Commissioners saw other picturesque rocks stencilled over with advertisements of patent medicines and found the walls of the Bower Cave, one of the most beautiful natural objects in the state, already so much broken and scratched by thoughtless visitors that it is evident that unless the practice should be prevented not many years will pass before its natural charms will be quite destroyed.

Second: it is important that it should be remembered that in permitting the sacrifice of anything that would be of the slightest value to future visitors to the convenience, bad taste, playfulness, carelessness, or wanton destructiveness of present visitors, we probably yield in each case the interest of uncounted millions to the selfishness of a few individuals.

It should, then, be made the duty of the Commission to prevent a wanton or careless disregard on the part of anyone entering the Yosemite or the Grove, of the rights of posterity as well as of contemporary visitors, and the Commission should be clothed with proper authority and given the necessary means for this purpose.

This duty of preservation is the first which falls upon the state under the Act of Congress, because the millions who are hereafter to benefit by the Act have the largest interest in it, and the largest interest should be first and most strenuously guarded.

James Bryce

SHOULD CARS BE ALLOWED IN YOSEMITE?

Bryce was a professor of civil law at Oxford, a Liberal M.P. for over a quarter-century, and, from 1907 to 1913, the British ambassador to the United States. Above all else, he was an inveterate student of the democratic process. He placed his formidable literary and conversational gifts (to those he met, he seemed "to have been everywhere, known everybody, and read everything") squarely in the service of his study. America, naturally, fascinated him. His masterwork, The American Commonwealth *(three volumes, published 1888), has been called by one historian "easily the most searching, most complete, most understanding analysis of American society by a Briton," his observations "matched only among all travelers to the United States by Tocqueville for originality and brilliance."*

That singularly democratic institution, the national park, did not escape Bryce's attention. Near the end of his tenure at Washington he delivered a series of addresses on diverse topics. One, entitled "National Parks—The Need of the Future," was made in 1912 before the annual convention of the influential American Civic Association, which was just then in the middle of a campaign to get the National Park Service established.

His address is an excellent example of that large class of national park literature devoted to admonishing the reader about an undesirable future.

After reading Bryce's counsel, anyone who has been to Yosemite Valley
at the height of summer will no doubt wish his words had been heeded.

As THE love of nature is happily increasing among us, it becomes all
the more important to find means for safeguarding nature. Population
is also increasing, and thus the number of people who desire to enjoy
nature is growing larger both absolutely and in proportion to the
whole. But, unfortunately, the opportunities for enjoyment, except
as regards easier locomotion, are not increasing. The world is circum-
scribed, and we feel the narrowness of it more and more as all its
corners are explored and surveyed. The surface of this little earth of
ours is indeed sadly limited, and we cannot add to it. When a man
finds his house too small, he builds more rooms on to it, but we cannot
add to our earth; we did not make it, it was made for us, and we cannot
by taking thought increase its dimensions. All that can be done is turn
it to the best possible account.

. . . Fortunately, you have made a good beginning in the work of
conservation. You have led the world in the creation of National Parks.
I have seen three or four of these, the Yosemite twice, the Yellowstone twice, and the splendid forest region around that mountain which
the people of Seattle now insist on calling Mount Rainier,—no doubt
the name originally given by Vancouver,—but which used, when I
wandered through its forests and traversed its glaciers, thirty years
ago, to be called by the more sonorous Indian name, Tacoma. And
there is also that superb reserve on the north side of the Grand Cañon
of the Colorado River, as well as Glacier Park in Montana and others
of minor extent in other parts of the country. The creation of such
National Parks has not only been good for you, but has had the admirable effect of setting other countries to emulate your example. Australia and New Zealand have followed that example. New Zealand,
in the district of its hot springs and geysers, has dedicated to the public
a scenic area something similar to your Yellowstone Park geyser region,
though not on so extensive a scale; the people of New South Wales
have set off three beautiful National Parks within forty miles of the
capital city of Sydney, taking mountain and forest regions of exquisite
beauty and keeping them for a source of delight to the growing population of that city. Thus your example is bearing good fruit. I only

Sentinel Rock

wish it had come sooner to us in England and Scotland before we had permitted the control of so much of our own best scenery to pass into private ownership.

One of the things your Association has to care for is not only the provision of more parks, but also the methods to be followed for keeping the existing parks in the best condition. I heard the other day that a question has been raised as to whether automobiles should be admitted in the Yosemite Valley. May a word be permitted on that subject? If Adam had known what harm the serpent was going to work, he would have tried to prevent him from finding lodgment in Eden; and if you stop to realize what the result of the automobile will be in that wonderful, that incomparable valley, you will keep it out. The one drawback to enjoyment of the Yosemite Valley in the summer and autumn is the dust. The granite rock becomes in the roads fine sand; even under existing conditions the feet of the horses and the wheels of the vehicles raise a great deal of it, enough to interfere with enjoyment as one drives or walks; but the conditions would become grievously worse with the swift automobile. And, further, the automobile would destroy what may be called the sentimental charm of the landscape. It is not merely that dust clouds would fill the air and coat the foliage, but the whole feeling of the spontaneity and freshness of primitive nature would be marred by this modern invention, with its din and whir and odious smell. Remember, moreover, that one cannot really enjoy fine scenery when travelling at a rate of fifteen to twenty or twenty-five miles an hour. If you want to enjoy the beauty of such landscapes as the Yosemite presents, you must see them slowly. Fine scenery is seen best of all in walking, when one can stop at any moment and enjoy any special point of view, but it is also agreeably seen in riding or driving, because in moving at a pace of five or six miles an hour you are not going too fast to take in the minor beauties of the landscape. But travelling faster than that—and my experience is that chauffeurs so delight in speed that it is hard to get them to slacken even when you bid them—you cannot enjoy the beauty. It was often my duty in the British Parliament to oppose bills conferring powers to build railways through some of the beautiful lake and valley scenery,—scenery on a much smaller scale than that of this Continent, but quite as beautiful, which we possess in Britain. The advocates of the bills urged that passengers could look out at the landscape from the windows of the railroad car. But we pointed out that it is impossible to get the full enjoyment of a romantic landscape from a railway window, especially where the beauties are delicate and the scale small. It is different where scenery is on a vast scale, so that the railway is insignificant in comparison, and the objects, rocks or mountains or rivers, are huge. There one may get some pleasure from the big views even as seen from a train, though they are far better seen in walking or driving, but you cannot enjoy the small beauties either of form or of colour. The focus is always changing, and it is impossible to give that kind of enjoyment which a painter, or any devotee of nature, seeks if you are hurrying past at a swift automobile pace. Whoever loves fine scenery has a sort of feeling that he is wasting it when he passes through it on a train instead of on foot or driving in an open vehicle.

It will of course be said that the automobile might be allowed to come up to the principal hotels and go no farther. If it is allowed to go so far as that, it will soon be allowed to go wherever else there is a road to bear it. Do not let the serpent enter Eden at all. Our friends who possess automobiles are numerous, wealthy, and powerful, but as all the rest of the North American Continent is open to them they are not gravely injured when one valley, besides parts of Mount Desert Island, is reserved for those who walk or ride. It is no intolerable hardship to be required to forgo in one spot a convenience which none of us had twenty years ago and which the great majority of our fellow-creatures cannot afford to pay for now. At present the railway comes to an end some twelve miles away from the entrance of the Yosemite Park, and the drive up to it behind horses gives far more pleasure than a journey by rail or motor car possibly could. There are plenty of roads elsewhere for lovers of speed and noise, without intruding on these few places where the wood nymphs and the water nymphs ought to be allowed to remain in untroubled seclusion, and their true worshippers to have the landscape to themselves.

Charles Dickens

THE FACTORIES
OF LOWELL

When hen Dickens alighted from the packet steamer Britannia *at the Custom House in Boston in early 1842, he was not yet thirty, but already famous as the author of the* Pickwick Papers, Oliver Twist, *and* Nicholas Nickleby, *among other novels. He had contracted with his publishers for a book of impressions of his American tour. He hoped for much from the United States; his mind's eye pictured a wholly enlightened nation. But fame cost him his chance to see the country on normal terms. Every day, free movement was foiled by rubber-neckers, glad-handers, and all other manner of the intrusively curious.* American Notes for General Circulation *is, considering the circumstances of his travels, a reasonable, measured account of what he saw, though colored by inevitable disappointment.*

Given Dickens's prepossessing interest in social issues and the laboring class, the town of Lowell, Massachusetts, was a natural for his itinerary. Incorporated in 1826, Lowell was devoted to the manufacture of textiles. The first city in the United States planned to take full advantage of the technology of the industrial revolution, Lowell also had a unique workforce (as Dickens will describe in this selection). For these reasons, Lowell National Historical Park was created in 1978.

Of all the towns Dickens saw, Lowell, at least, lived up to his expectations. "I assign a separate chapter to this visit," he explained in American Notes, *"not because I am about to describe it at any length, but because I remember it as a thing by itself, and am desirous that my readers should do the same." Later he said that his day in Lowell was the happiest he had spent in America.*

I WAS met at the station at Lowell by a gentleman intimately connected with the management of the factories there; and gladly putting myself under his guidance, drove off at once to that quarter of the town in which the works, the object of my visit, were situated. Although only just of age—for if my recollection serve me, it has been a manufacturing town barely one-and-twenty years—Lowell is a large, populous, thriving place. Those indications of its youth which first attract the eye, give it a quaintness and oddity of character which, to a visitor from the old country, is amusing enough. It was a very dirty winter's day, and nothing in the whole town looked old to me, except the mud, which in some parts was almost knee-deep, and might have been deposited there on the subsiding of the waters after the Deluge. In one place, there was a new wooden church, which, having no steeple, and being yet unpainted, looked like an enormous packing-case without any direction upon it. In another there was a large hotel, whose walls and colonnades were so crisp, and thin, and slight, that it had exactly the appearance of being built with cards. I was careful not to draw my breath as we passed, and trembled when I saw a workman come out upon the roof, lest with one thoughtless stamp of his foot he should crush the structure beneath him, and bring it rattling down. The very river that moves the machinery in the mills (for they are all worked by water power), seems to acquire a new character from the fresh buildings of bright red brick and painted wood among which it takes its course; and to be as light-headed, thoughtless, and brisk a young river, in its murmurings and tumblings, as one would desire to see. One would swear that every "Bakery," "Grocery," and "Bookbindery," and other kind of store, took its shutters down for the first time, and started in business yesterday. The golden pestles and mortars fixed as signs upon the sun blind frames outside the druggist's, appear to have been just turned out of the United States' Mint; and when I saw a baby of some week or ten days old in a woman's arms at a street corner, I found myself unconsciously wondering where it came from: never supposing for an instant that it could have been born in such a young town as that.

There are several factories in Lowell, each of which belongs to what we should term a Company of Proprietors, but what they call in America a Corporation. I went over several of these; such as a woolen factory, a carpet factory, and a cotton factory: examined them in every part; and saw them in their ordinary working aspect, with no preparation of any kind, or departure from their ordinary every-day proceedings. I may add that I am well acquainted with our manufacturing towns in England, and have visited many mills in Manchester and elsewhere in the same manner.

I happened to arrive at the first factory just as the dinner-hour was over, and the girls were returning to their work; indeed, the stairs of the mill were thronged with them as I ascended. They were all well-dressed, but not to my thinking above their condition: for I like to see the humbler classes of society careful of their dress and appearance, and even, if they please, decorated with such little trinkets as come within the compass of their means. Supposing it confined within reasonable limits, I would always encourage this kind of pride as a worthy element of self-respect, in any person I employed; and should no more be deterred from doing so, because some wretched female referred her fall to a love of dress, than I would allow my construction of the real intent and meaning of the Sabbath to be influenced by any warning to the well-disposed, founded on his back-slidings on that particular day, which might emanate from the rather doubtful authority of a murderer in Newgate.

These girls, as I have said, were all well dressed: and that phrase necessarily includes extreme cleanliness. They had serviceable bonnets, good warm cloaks, and shawls; and were not above clogs and pattens. Moreover, there were places in the mill in which they could deposit these things without injury; and there were conveniences for washing. They were healthy in appearance, many of them remarkably so, and had the manners and deportment of young women: not of degraded brutes of burden. If I had seen in one of those mills (but I did not, though I looked for something of this kind with a sharp eye), the most lisping, mincing, affected, and ridiculous young creature that my imagination could suggest, I should have thought of the careless, moping, slatternly, degraded, dull reverse (I *have* seen that), and should have been still well pleased to look upon her.

The rooms in which they worked were as well ordered as themselves. In the windows of some there were green plants, which were trained to shade the glass; in all, there was as much fresh air, cleanliness, and comfort as the nature of the occupation would possibly admit of. Out of so large a number of females, many of whom were only then just verging upon womanhood, it may be reasonably supposed that some were delicate and fragile in appearance: no doubt there were. But I solemnly declare, that from all the crowd I saw in the different factories that day, I cannot recall or separate one young face that gave me a painful impression; not one young girl whom, assuming it to be a matter of necessity that she should gain her daily bread by the labour of her hands, I would have removed from those works if I had had the power.

They reside at various boarding-houses near at hand. The owners of the mills are particularly careful to allow no persons to enter upon the possession of these houses, whose characters have not undergone the most searching and thorough inquiry. Any complaint that is made against them by the boarders or by anybody else, is fully investigated; and if good ground of complaint be shown to exist against them, they are removed, and their occupation is handed over to some more deserving person. There are a few children employed in these factories, but not many. The laws of the State forbid their working more than nine months in the year, and require that they be educated during the other three. For this purpose there are schools in Lowell; and there are churches and chapels of various persuasions, in which the young women may observe that form of Worship in which they have been educated.

At some distance from the factories, and on the highest and pleasantest ground in the neighbourhood, stands their hospital, or boarding-house for the sick: it is the best house in those parts, and was built by an eminent merchant for his own residence. Like that institution at Boston which I have before described, it is not parcelled out into wards, but is divided into convenient chambers, each of which has all the comforts of a very comfortable home. The principal medical attendant resides under the same roof; and were the patients members of his own family, they could not be better cared for, or attended with greater gentleness and consideration. The weekly charge in this establishment for each patient is three dollars, or twelve shillings English; but no girl employed by any of the corporations is ever excluded for want of the means of payment. That they do not very often want the means, may be gathered from the fact, that in July, 1841, no fewer than nine hundred and seventy-eight of these girls were depositors in the Lowell Savings Bank: the amount of whose joint savings was estimated at one hundred thousand dollars, or twenty thousand English pounds.

I am now going to state three facts, which will startle a large class of readers on this side of the Atlantic, very much.

Firstly, there is a joint-stock piano in a great many of the boarding-houses. Secondly, nearly all these young ladies subscribe to circulating libraries. Thirdly, they have got up among themselves a periodical called *The Lowell Offering*, "A repository of original articles, written exclusively by females actively employed in the mills," which is duly printed, published, and sold; and whereof I brought away from Lowell four hundred good solid pages, which I have read from beginning to end.

The large class of readers, startled by these facts will exclaim, with one voice, "How very preposterous!" On my deferentially inquiring why, they will answer, "These things are above their station." In reply to that objection, I would beg to ask what their station is.

It is their station to work. And they *do* work. They labour in these mills, upon an average, twelve hours a day, which is unquestionably work, and pretty tight work too. Perhaps it is above their station to indulge in such amusements, on any terms. Are we quite sure that we in England have not formed our ideas of the "station" of working people, from accustoming ourselves to the contemplation of that class as they are, and not as they might be? I think that if we examine our own feelings, we shall find that the pianos, and the circulating-libraries, and even *The Lowell Offering*, startle us by their novelty, and not by their bearing upon any abstract question of right and wrong.

For myself, I know no station in which, the occupation of to-day cheerfully done and the occupation of to-morrow cheerfully looked to, any one of these pursuits is not most humanizing and laudable. I know no station which is rendered more endurable to the person in it, or more safe to the person out of it, by having ignorance for its associate. I know no station which has a right to monopolize the means of mutual instruction, improvement, and rational entertainment or which has ever continued to be a station very long, after seeking to do so.

Lowell, Massachusetts as Charles Dickens might have found it

Of the merits of *The Lowell Offering* as a literary production, I will only observe, putting entirely out of sight the fact of the articles having been written by these girls after the arduous labours of the day, that it will compare advantageously with a great many English Annuals. It is pleasant to find that many of its Tales are of the Mills and of those who work in them; that they inculcate habits of self-denial and contentment, and teach doctrines of enlarged benevolence. A strong feeling for the beauties of nature, as displayed in the solitudes the writers have left at home, breathes through its pages like wholesome village air; and though a circulating library is a favourable school for the study of such topics, it has very scanty allusion to fine clothes, fine marriages, fine homes, or fine life. Some persons might object to the papers being signed occasionally with rather fine names, but this is an American fashion. One of the provinces of the state legislature of Massachusetts is to alter ugly names into pretty ones, as the children improve upon the tastes of their parents. These changes costing little or nothing, scores of Mary Annes are solemnly converted into Bevelinas every session.

It is said that on the occasion of a visit from General Jackson or General Harrison to this town (I forget which, but it is not to the purpose), he walked through three miles and a half of these young ladies, all dressed out with parasols and silk stockings. But as I am not aware that any worse consequence ensued, than a sudden looking-up of all the parasols and silk stockings in the market; and perhaps the bankruptcy of some speculative New-Englander who bought them all up at one price, in expectation of a demand that never came; I set no great store by the circumstance.

In this brief account of Lowell, and inadequate expression of the gratification it yielded me, and cannot fail to afford to any foreigner to whom the condition of such people at home is a subject of interest and anxious speculation, I have carefully abstained from drawing a comparison between these factories and those of our own land. Many of the circumstances whose strong influence has been at work for years in our manufacturing towns have not arisen here; and there is no manufacturing population in Lowell, so to speak: for these girls (often the daughters of small farmers) come from other states, remain a few years in the mills, and then go home for good.

The contrast would be a strong one, for it would be between the Good and Evil, the living light and deepest shadow. I abstain from it, because I deem it just to do so. But I only the more earnestly adjure all those whose eyes may rest upon these pages, to pause and reflect upon the difference between this town and those great haunts of desperate misery: to call to mind, if they can in the midst of party strife and squabble, the efforts that must be made to purge them of their suffering and danger: and last, and foremost, to remember how the precious Time is rushing by.

Bayard Taylor

A SECOND WORLD

It is not possible for the modern reader to accurately gauge the reputation Bayard Taylor built during his lifetime. His many books of travel, as well as novels, short stories, and poetry, made him better known and more admired than, say, Walt Whitman—both by the public and by a significant portion of the literary establishment. Upon reading Taylor today, one cannot figure out why. Even his most recent biographer, who gives him every benefit of the doubt, concedes not much of his work is worth preserving. What Taylor did, though, and did admirably, was fulfill the expectations of mid-nineteeth-century readers.

Taylor was perhaps the most widely traveled American of his time. He made the usual itineraries seem different, as when he took a two-year walk around Europe. He also veered well off the beaten path, from Iceland to central Africa. In all, Taylor made extensive trips to every continent except Australia, and though he wanted to be remembered for his fiction and poetry, he spent most of his career describing the rest of the world to a rapt United States.

Some of his best prose, however, is devoted to American places. In mid-century, before the marvels of Yellowstone and Yosemite had become widely known (and believed), the three great scenic wonders in the United States were Niagara Falls, the natural bridge near Lexington, Virginia, and

*Mammoth Cave in Kentucky. Of these, only Mammoth Cave has become
a national park. Taylor's description of the cave, based on trips he made
in 1855, is notable as a record of how one's perception becomes distorted
in an unusual environment—a phenomenon we will meet again in the
next selection.*

THERE WAS no outbreathing from the regions below as we stood at
the entrance to the cave, the upper atmosphere having precisely the
same temperature. We advanced single file down the Main Avenue,
which, from the increased number of lamps, showed with greater dis-
tinctness than on our first trip. Without pausing at any of the objects
of interest on the road, we marched to the Giant's Coffin, crawled
through the hole behind it, passed the Deserted Chambers, and reached
the Bottomless Pit, the limit of our journey in this direction the previous day.

Beyond the Pit we entered upon new ground. After passing from
under its Moorish dome the ceiling became low and the path sinuous
and rough. I could only walk by stooping considerably, and it is necessary to keep a sharp look-out to avoid striking your head against the
transverse jambs of rock. This passage is aptly called the Valley of
Humiliation. It branches off to the right into another passage called
Pensico Avenue, which contains some curious stalactitic formations,
similar to the Gothic Gallery. We did not explore it, but turned to
the left and entered an extremely narrow, winding passage, which
meanders through the solid rock. It is called Fat Man's Misery, and
any one whose body is more than eighteen inches in breadth will have
trouble to get through. The largest man who ever passed it weighed
two hundred and sixty pounds, and any gentleman weighing more
than that must leave the best part of the cave unexplored. None of
us came within the scope of prohibition (Nature, it seems, is opposed
to corpulence), and after five minutes' twisting we emerged into a
spacious hall called the Great Relief. Its continuation forms an avenue
which leads to Bandits' Hall—a wild, rugged vault, the bottom of which
is heaped with huge rocks that have fallen from above. All this part
of the cave is rich in striking and picturesque effects, and presents a
more rude and irregular character than anything we had yet seen.

"Fat Man's Misery"

At the end of Bandits' Hall is the Meat-Room, where a fine collection of limestone hams and shoulders are suspended from the ceiling, as in a smoke-house; the resemblance, which is really curious, is entirely owing to the action of the water. The air now grew perceptibly damp, and a few more steps brought us to the entrance of River Hall. Here the ceiling not only becomes loftier, but the floor gradually slopes away from you, and you look down into the vast depths and uncertain darkness, and question yourself if the Grecian fable be not indeed true. While I paused on the brink of these fresh mysteries the others of the party had gone ahead under the charge of Mat; Stephen, who remained with me, proposed that we should descend to the banks of the Styx and see them crossing the river upon the Natural Bridge. We stood on the brink of the black, silent water; the arch of the portal was scarcely visible in the obscurity far above us. Now, as far below, I saw the twinkle of a distant lamp, then another and another. "Is it possible," I asked, "that they have descended so much further?" "You forget," said Stephen, "that you are looking into the river and see their reflected images. Stoop a little and you will find that they are high above the water." I stooped and looked under an arch, and saw the slow procession of golden points of light passing over the gulf under the eaves of a great cliff; but another procession quite as distinct passed on below until the last lamp disappeared and all was darkness again.

Five minutes more and the roughest and most slippery scrambling brought us to the banks of the Lethe River, where we found the rest of the party.

The river had risen since the previous day, and was at the most inconvenient stage possible. A part of the River Walk was overflowed, yet not deep enough to float the boats. Mat waded out and turned the craft, which was moored to a projecting rock, as near to us as the water would allow, after which he and Stephen carried us one by one upon their shoulders and deposited us in it. It was a rude, square scow, well plastered with river mud. Boards were laid across for the ladies, the rest of us took our seats on the muddy gunwales, the guides plied their paddles, and we were afloat on Lethe.

After a ferriage of about one hundred yards, we landed on a bank of soft mud beside a small arm of the river, which had overflowed the usual path. We sank to our ankles in the moist tenacious soil, floundering laboriously along until we were brought to a halt by Echo River, the third and last stream. This again is divided into three or four arms, which, meandering away under low arches, finally unite.

As we stood on the wet rocks, peering down into the black translucence of the silent, mysterious water, sounds—first distant, then near, then distant again— stole to us from under the groined vaults of rock.

First, the dip of many oars; then a dull, muffled peal, rumbling away like the echoes of thunder; then a voice marvelously sweet, but presently joined by others sweeter still, taking up the dying notes ere they faded into silence, and prolonging them through remoter chambers. The full, mellow strains rose until they seemed sung at our very ears, then relapsed like ebbing waves, to wander off into solitary halls, then approached again, and receded, like lost spirits seeking here and there for an outlet from the world of darkness. Or was it a chorus of angels come on some errand of pity and mercy to visit the Stygian shores? As the heavenly harmonies thickened, we saw a gleam on the water, and presently a clear light, floating above its mirrored counterfeit, swept into sight. It was no angel, but Stephen, whose single voice had been multiplied into that enchanting chorus. . . .

. . . Nearly five hours had now elapsed since we entered the cave, and five hours spent in that bracing, stimulating atmosphere might well justify the longing glances which we cast upon the baskets carried by the guides. Mr. Miller had foreseen our appetites, and there were stores of venison, biscuit, ham, and pastry, more than sufficient for all. We made our midday, or rather midnight, meal sitting, like the nymph who wrought Excalibur "Upon the hidden bases of the hills," buried far below the green Kentucky forests, far below the forgotten sunshine. For in the cave you forget that there is an outer world somewhere above you. The hours have no meaning: Time ceases to be; no thought of labour, no sense of responsibility, no twinge of conscience intrudes to suggest the existence you have left. You walk in some limbo beyond the confines of actual life, yet no nearer the world of spirits. For my part, I could not shake off the impression that I was wandering on the *outside* of Uranus or Neptune, or some planet still more deeply buried in the frontier darkness of our solar system. . . .

We retraced our steps slowly along Elindo Avenue, stopping every few minutes to take a last look at the bowers of fairy blossoms. After reaching Washington's Hall we noticed that the air was no longer still, but was flowing fresh and cool in our faces. Stephen observed it also, and said: "There has been a heavy rain outside." Entering the pass of El Ghor again at Martha's Vineyard, we walked rapidly forward, without making a halt, to its termination at Silliman's Avenue. The distance is reckoned by the guides at a little more than a mile and a half, and we were just forty minutes in walking it. We several times felt fatigue, especially when passing the rougher parts of the cave, but the

Scenes in Mammoth Cave

sensation always passed away in some unaccountable manner, leaving us fresh and buoyant. The crossing of the rivers was accomplished with some labour, but without accident. I accompanied Stephen on his return through the second arch of Echo River. As I sat alone in the silent, transparent darkness of the mysterious stream, I could hear the tones of my boatman's voice gliding down the caverns like a wave, flowing more and more faintly until its vibrations were too weak to move the ear. Thus, as he sang, there were frequently three or four notes, each distinctly audible, floating away at different degrees of remoteness. At the last arch there was only a space of eighteen inches between the water and the rock. We lay down on our backs in the muddy bottom of the boat, and squeezed through to the middle branch of the Echo River, where we found the rest of the party, who had gone around through Purgatory. After again threading Fat Man's Misery, passing the Bottomless Pit and the Deserted Chambers, we at last emerged into the Main Avenue at the Giant's Coffin. It was six o'clock, and we had been ten hours in the cave.

When we heard the tinkling drops of the little cascade over the entrance, I looked up and saw a patch of deep, tender blue set in the darkness. In the midst of it twinkled a white star—whiter and more dazzling than any star I ever saw before. I paused and drank at the trough under the waterfall, for, like the Fountain of Trevi at Rome, it may be that those who drink there shall return again. When we ascended to the level of the upper world we found that a fierce tornado had passed along during the day; trees had been torn up by the roots and hurled down in all directions; stunning thunders had jarred the air, and the wet earth was fairly paved with leaves cut off by the heavy hail—yet we, buried in the heart of the hills, had heard no sound, nor felt the slightest tremour in the air.

The stars were all in their places as I walked back to the hotel. I had been twelve hours under ground, in which I had walked about twenty-four miles. I had lost a day—a day with its joyous morning, its fervid noon, its tempest, and its angry sunset of crimson and gold; but I had gained an age in a strange and hitherto unknown world—an age of wonderful experience, and an exhaustless store of sublime and lovely memories.

Mark Twain

THE HAWAII VOLCANOES

*B*oth literary critics and the reading public have long held Mark Twain's Roughing It *to be in the choice of his writing. The book, for the most part a humorous work of fiction, draws upon his Western experience of the 1860s. Samuel Clemens first went to the West in the summer of 1861 with his brother Orion, who had just been appointed Secretary of Nevada Territory. Clemens spent the next few years as a newspaperman in Nevada and California. In 1866, he sailed for the Sandwich Islands—today's Hawaii—as a special correspondent for the Sacramento Union. His island letters are, according to Bernard De Voto, in the "highest reach of his California period," with passages of eloquence that equal any to be found in his travel books.*

Mark Twain's original plan for Roughing It *did not include an account of the islands. But he was so fond of a character sketch of an inveterate liar he had met on Maui that he decided to work Hawaii into the book.* Roughing It *has a full account of Clemens's visit to two of the greatest Hawaiian volcanoes. One, Kilauea, still very much alive, is part of Hawaii Volcanoes National Park. The other, Haleakala, has long been dormant. Its crater is the centerpiece of Haleakala National Park on Maui.*

WE GOT back to the schooner in good time, and then sailed down to
Kau, where we disembarked and took final leave of the vessel. Next
day we bought horses and bent our way over the summer-clad moun-
tain-terraces, toward the great volcano of Kilauea (Ke-low-way-ah).
We made nearly a two days' journey of it, but that was on account of
laziness. Toward sunset on the second day, we reached an elevation
of some four thousand feet above sea level, and as we picked our careful
way through billowy wastes of lava long generations ago stricken dead
and cold in the climax of its tossing fury, we began to come upon
signs of the near presence of the volcano—signs in the nature of ragged
fissures that discharged jets of sulphurous vapor into the air, hot from
the molten ocean down in the bowels of the mountain.

Shortly the crater came into view. I have seen Vesuvius since, but
it is a mere toy, a child's volcano, a soup-kettle, compared to this.
Mount Vesuvius is a shapely cone thirty-six hundred feet high; its crater
an inverted cone only three hundred feet deep, and not more than
a thousand feet in diameter, if as much as that; its fires meagre, modest,
and docile. But here was a vast, perpendicular, walled cellar, nine
hundred feet deep in some places, thirteen hundred in others, level-
floored, and *ten miles in circumference!* Here was a yawning pit upon
whose floor the armies of Russia could camp, and have room to spare.

Perched upon the edge of the crater, at the opposite end from where
we stood, was a small lookout house—say three miles away. It assisted
us, by comparison, to comprehend and appreciate the great depth of
the basin—it looked like a tiny martin-box clinging at the eaves of
a cathedral. After some little time spent in resting and looking and
ciphering, we hurried on to the hotel.

By the path it is half a mile from the Volcano House to the lookout
house. After a hearty supper we waited until it was thoroughly dark
and then started to the crater. The first glance in that direction revealed
a scene of wild beauty. There was a heavy fog over the crater and
it was splendidly illuminated by the glare from the fires below. The
illumination was two miles wide and a mile high, perhaps; and if you
ever, on a dark night and at a distance beheld the light from thirty
or forty blocks of distant buildings all on fire at once, reflected strongly
against the overhanging clouds, you can form a fair idea of what this
looked like.

A colossal column of cloud towered to a great height in the air immediately above the crater, and the outer swell of every one of its vast

Mark Twain about the time of his visit to Hawaii

folds was dyed with a rich crimson lustre, which was subdued to a
pale rose tint in the depressions between. It glowed like a muffled torch
and stretched upward to a dizzy height toward the zenith. I thought
it just possible that its like had not been seen since the children of
Israel wandered on their long march through the desert so many centuries ago over a path illuminated by the mysterious "pillar of fire."
And I was sure that I now had a vivid conception of what the majestic
"pillar of fire" was like, which almost amounted to a revelation.

Arrived at the little thatched lookout house, we rested our elbows
on the railing in front and looked abroad over the wide crater and
down over the sheer precipice at the seething fires beneath us. The
view was a startling improvement on my daylight experience. I turned
to see the effect on the balance of the company and found the reddest-
faced set of men I almost ever saw. In the strong light every counte-
nance glowed like red-hot iron, every shoulder was suffused with
crimson and shaded rearward into dingy, shapeless obscurity! The place
below looked like the infernal regions and these men like half-cooled
devils just come up on a furlough.

I turned my eyes upon the volcano again. The "cellar" was tolerably
well lighted up. For a mile and a half in front of us and half a mile
on either side, the floor of the abyss was magnificently illuminated;
beyond these limits the mists hung down their gauzy curtains and
cast a deceptive gloom over all that made the twinkling fires in the
remote corners of the crater seem countless leagues removed—made
them seem like the camp-fires of a great army far away. Here was room
for the imagination to work! You could imagine those lights the width
of a continent away—and that hidden under the intervening darkness
were hills, and winding rivers, and weary wastes of plain and desert—
and even then the tremendous vista stretched on, and on, and on!—to
the fires and far beyond! You could not compass it—it was the idea
of eternity made tangible—and the longest end of it made visible to
the naked eye!

The greater part of the vast floor of the desert under us was as black
as ink, and apparently smooth and level; but over a mile square of
it was ringed and streaked and striped with a thousand branching
streams of liquid and gorgeously brilliant fire! It looked like a colossal
railroad map of the State of Massachusetts done in chain lightning
on a midnight sky. Imagine it—imagine a coal-black sky shivered into
a tangled net-work of angry fire!

Here and there were gleaming holes a hundred feet in diameter, broken in the dark crust, and in them the melted lava–the color a dazzling white just tinged with yellow–was boiling and surging furiously; and from these holes branched numberless bright torrents in many directions, like the spokes of a wheel, and kept a tolerably straight course for a while and then swept round in huge rainbow curves, or made a long succession of sharp worm-fence angles, which looked precisely like the fiercest jagged lightning. These streams met other streams, and they mingled with and crossed and recrossed each other in every conceivable direction, like skate tracks on a popular skating ground. Sometimes streams twenty or thirty feet wide flowed from the holes to some distance without dividing–and through the opera-glasses we could see that they ran down small, steep hills and were genuine cataracts of fire, white at their source, but soon cooling and turning to the richest red, grained with alternate lines of black and gold. Every now and then masses of the dark crust broke away and floated slowly down these streams like rafts down a river. Occasionally the molten lava flowing under the superincumbent crust broke through–split a dazzling streak, from five hundred to a thousand feet long, like a sudden flash of lightning, and then acre after acre of the cold lava parted into fragments, turned up edgewise like cakes of ice when a great river breaks up, plunged downward and were swallowed in the crimson cauldron. Then the wide expanse of the "thaw" maintained a ruddy glow for a while, but shortly cooled and became black and level again. During a "thaw," every dismembered cake was marked by a glittering white border which was superbly shaded inward by aurora borealis rays, which were a flaming yellow where they joined the white border, and from thence toward their points tapered into a glowing crimson, then into a rich, pale carmine, and finally into a faint blush that held its own a moment and then dimmed and turned black. Some of the streams preferred to mingle together in a tangle of fantastic circles, and then they looked something like the confusion of ropes one sees on a ship's deck when she has just taken in sail and dropped anchor–provided one can imagine those ropes on fire.

Through the glasses, the little fountains scattered about looked very beautiful. They boiled, and coughed, and spluttered, and discharged sprays of stringy red fire–of about the consistency of mush, for instance –from ten to fifteen feet into the air, along with a shower of brilliant white sparks–a quaint and unnatural mingling of gouts of blood and snow-flakes!

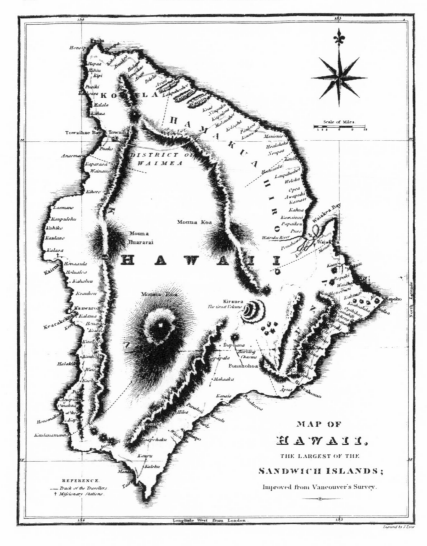

We had circles and serpents and streaks of lightning all twined and
wreathed and tied together, without a break throughout an area more
than a mile square (that amount of ground was covered, though it
was not strictly "square"), and it was with a feeling of placid exulta-
tion that we reflected that many years had elapsed since any visitor
had seen such a splendid display—since any visitor had seen anything

more than the now snubbed and insignificant "North" and "South" lakes in action. We had been reading old files of Hawaiian newspapers and the "Record Book" at the Volcano House, and were posted.

I could see the North Lake lying out on the black floor away off in the outer edge of our panorama, and knitted to it by a web-work of lava streams. In its individual capacity it looked very little more respectable than a schoolhouse on fire. True, it was about nine hundred feet long and two or three hundred wide, but then, under the present circumstances, it necessarily appeared rather insignificant, and besides it was so distant from us.

I forgot to say that the noise made by the bubbling lava is not great, heard as we heard it from our lofty perch. It makes three distinct sounds—a rushing, a hissing, and a coughing or puffing sound; and if you stand on the brink and close your eyes it is no trick at all to imagine that you are sweeping down a river on a large low-pressure steamer, and that you hear the hissing of the steam about her boilers, the puffing from her escape-pipes and the churning push of the water abaft her wheels. The smell of sulphur is strong, but not unpleasant to a sinner.

We left the lookout house at ten o'clock in a half cooked condition, because of the heat from Pele's furnaces, and wrapping up in blankets, for the night was cold, we returned to our hotel.

The next night was appointed for a visit to the bottom of the crater, for we desired to traverse its floor and see the "North Lake" (of fire) which lay two miles away, toward the further wall. After dark half a dozen of us set out, with lanterns and native guides, and climbed down a crazy, thousand-foot pathway in a crevice fractured in the crater-wall, and reached the bottom in safety.

The eruption of the previous evening had spent its force and the floor looked black and cold; but when we ran out upon it we found it hot yet, to the feet, and it was likewise riven with crevices which revealed the underlying fires gleaming vindictively. A neighboring cauldron was threatening to overflow, and this added to the dubiousness of the situation. So the native guides refused to continue the venture, and then everybody deserted except a stranger named Marlette. He said he had been in the crater a dozen times in daylight and believed he could find his way through it at night. He thought that a run of three hundred yards would carry us over the hottest part of the floor and leave us our shoe-soles. His pluck gave me back-bone. We took one lantern and instructed the guides to hang the other to the roof of the lookout house to serve as a beacon for us in case we got lost, and then the party started back up the precipice and Marlette and I made our run. We skipped over the hot floor and over the red crevices with brisk dispatch and reached the cold lava safe but with pretty warm feet. Then we took things leisurely and comfortably, jumping tolerably wide and probably bottomless chasms, and threading our way through picturesque lava upheavals with considerable confidence. When we got fairly away from the cauldron of boiling fire, we seemed to be in a gloomy desert, and a suffocatingly dark one, surrounded by dim walls that seemed to tower to the sky. The only cheerful objects were the glinting stars high overhead.

By and by Marlette shouted "Stop!" I never stopped quicker in my life. I asked what the matter was. He said we were out of the path. He said we must not try to go on till we found it again, for we were surrounded with beds of rotten lava through which we could easily break and plunge down a thousand feet. I thought eight hundred would answer for me, and was about to say so when Marlette partly proved his statement by accidentally crushing through and disappearing to his arm-pits. He got out and we hunted for the path with the lantern. He said there was only one path and that it was but vaguely defined. We could not find it. The lava surface was all alike in the lantern light. But he was an ingenious man. He said it was not the lantern that had informed him that we were out of the path, but his *feet*. He had noticed a crisp grinding of fine lava-needles under his feet, and some instinct reminded him that in the path these were all worn away. So he put his lantern behind him, and began to search with his boots instead of his eyes. It was good sagacity. The first time his foot touched a surface that did not grind under it he announced that the trail was found again; and after that we kept up a sharp listening for the rasping sound and it always warned us in time.

It was a long tramp, but an exciting one. We reached the North Lake between ten and eleven o'clock, and sat down on a huge overhanging lava-shelf, tired but satisfied. The spectacle presented was worth coming double the distance to see. Under us, and stretching away before us, was a heaving sea of molten fire of seemingly limitless extent. The glare from it was so blinding that it was some time before we could bear to look upon it steadily. It was like gazing at the sun at noonday,

except that the glare was not quite so white. At unequal distances all
around the shores of the lake were nearly white-hot chimneys or
hollow drums of lava, four or five feet high, and up through them
were bursting gorgeous sprays of lava-gouts and gem spangles, some
white, some red and some golden—a ceaseless bombardment, and one
that fascinated the eye with its unapproachable splendor. The more
distant jets, sparkling up through an intervening gossamer veil of vapor,
seemed miles away; and the further the curving ranks of fiery mountains receded, the more fairy-like and beautiful they appeared.

Now and then the surging bosom of the lake under our noses would
calm down ominously and seem to be gathering strength for an enterprise; and then all of a sudden a red dome of lava of the bulk of an
ordinary dwelling would heave itself aloft like an escaping balloon,
then burst asunder, and out of its heart would flit a pale-green film
of vapor, and float upward and vanish in the darkness—a released soul
soaring homeward from captivity with the damned, no doubt. The
crashing plunge of the ruined dome into the lake again would send

a world of seething billows lashing against the shores and shaking the foundations of our perch. By and by, a loosened mass of the hanging shelf we sat on tumbled into the lake, jarring the surroundings like an earthquake and delivering a suggestion that may have been intended for a hint, and may not. We did not wait to see.

We got lost again on our way back, and were more than an hour hunting for the path. We were where we could see the beacon lantern at the lookout house at the time, but thought it was a star and paid no attention to it. We reached the hotel at two o'clock in the morning pretty well fagged out.

. . . The chief pride of Maui is her dead volcano of Haleakala—which means, translated, "the house of the sun." We climbed a thousand feet up the side of this isolated colossus one afternoon; then camped, and next day climbed the remaining nine thousand feet, and anchored on the summit, where we built a fire and froze and roasted by turns, all night. With the first pallor of dawn we got up and saw things that were new to us. Mounted on a commanding pinnacle, we watched Nature work her silent wonders. The sea was spread abroad on every hand, its tumbled surface seeming only wrinkled and dimpled in the distance. A broad valley below appeared like an ample checker-board, its velvety green sugar plantations alternating with dun squares of barrenness and groves of trees diminished to mossy tufts. Beyond the valley were mountains picturesquely grouped together; but bear in mind, we fancied that we were looking *up* at these things—not down. We seemed to sit at the bottom of a symmetrical bowl ten thousand feet deep, with the valley and the skirting sea lifted away into the sky above us! It was curious; and not only curious, but aggravating; for it was having our trouble all for nothing, to climb ten thousand feet toward heaven and then have to look *up* at our scenery. However, we had to be content with it and make the best of it; for, all we could do we could not coax our landscape down out of the clouds. Formerly, when I had read an article in which Poe treated this singular fraud perpetrated upon the eye by isolated great altitudes, I had looked upon the matter as an invention of his own fancy.

I have spoken of the outside view—but we had an inside one, too. That was the yawning dead crater, into which we now and then tumbled rocks, half as large as a barrel, from our perch, and saw them go crashing down the almost perpendicular sides, bounding three hundred feet at a jump; kicking up dust-clouds wherever they struck; diminishing to our view as they sped farther into distance; growing invisible, finally, and only betraying their course by faint little puffs of dust; and coming to a halt at last in the bottom of the abyss, two thousand five hundred feet down from they started! It was magnificent sport. We wore ourselves out at it.

The crater of Vesuvius, as I have before remarked, is a modest pit about a thousand feet deep and three thousand in circumference; that of Kilauea is somewhat deeper, and *ten miles* in circumference. But what are either of them compared to the vacant stomach of Haleakala? I will not offer any figures of my own, but give official ones—those of Commander Wilkes, U.S.N., who surveyed it and testifies that it is *twenty-seven miles in circumference!* If it had a level bottom it would make a fine site for a city like London. It must have afforded a spectacle worth contemplating in the old days when its furnaces gave full rein to their anger.

Presently vagrant white clouds came drifting along, high over the sea and the valley; then they came in couples and groups; then in imposing squadrons; gradually joining their forces, they banked themselves solidly together, a thousand feet under us, and *totally shut out land and ocean*—not a vestige of *anything* was left in view but just a little rim of the crater, circling away from the pinnacle whereon we sat (for a ghostly procession of wanderers from the filmy hosts without had drifted through a chasm in the crater wall and filed round and round, and gathered and sunk and blended together till the abyss was stored to the brim with fleecy fog). Thus banked, motion ceased, and silence reigned. Clear to the horizon, league on league, the snowy floor stretched without a break—not level, but in rounded folds, with shallow creases between, and with here and there stately piles of vapory architecture lifting themselves aloft out of the common plain—some near at hand, some in the middle distances, and others relieving the monotony of the remote solitudes. There was little conversation, for the impressive scene overawed speech. I felt like the Last Man, neglected of the judgment, and left pinnacled in mid-heaven, a forgotten relic of a vanished world.

While the hush yet brooded, the messengers of the coming resurrection appeared in the east. A growing warmth suffused the horizon, and soon the sun emerged and looked out over the cloud-waste, flinging bars of ruddy light across it, staining its folds and billow-caps with blushes, purpling the shaded troughs between, and glorifying the massy vapor-palaces and cathedrals with a wasteful splendor of all blendings and combinations of rich coloring.

It was the sublimest spectacle I ever witnessed, and I think the memory of it will remain with me always.

Wallace Stegner

THE MARKS OF
HUMAN PASSAGE

No one could have foreseen that the most virulent conservation battle of the 1950s—indeed, since Hetch Hetchy forty years before—would be fought over the fate of remote canyons in an obscure national monument. Until 1950, few people had heard of Dinosaur National Monument, let alone the plans of the Bureau of Reclamation to build a dam at Echo Park (the junction of the Green and Yampa rivers) in the Colorado portion of Dinosaur. Then, that July, Bernard De Voto broadcast the Bureau's cost-benefit figures in a Saturday Evening Post *article and, for the further edification of the public, shot holes in them. In November another opinion-leading magazine,* Reader's Digest, *reprinted the article. Suddenly millions of people had heard of Dinosaur and Echo Park. Buoyed by the public's new-found concern, conservationists organized to thwart the dam.*

The writer Wallace Stegner, who had been a friend of De Voto's since 1939, soon joined the cause. Stegner's interest was natural: he was just finishing his path-breaking history of the career of John Wesley Powell, who had explored Echo Park on his way to the Grand Canyon. At the urging of the Sierra Club's David Brower, Stegner edited a call-to-arms entitled This is Dinosaur: Echo Park Country and its Magic Rivers. *This, the first of the Club's "fighting books," was put out in 1955 by the publishing house of Alfred A. Knopf, whose namesake had himself been*

a strong supporter of the national parks ever since De Voto arranged a
tour of the West for him seven years before. Stegner also wrote the first
chapter of This is Dinosaur, *a summary of the exploration of the*
canyons—and a reminder of what would be lost if the dam were built.
A copy of the book was sent to every Senator and Representative. Later
that year Congress finally quashed the dam plans. Echo Park was a complete
victory for the conservationists. More than that, it marked their coming
of age as a political force.

DINOSAUR NATIONAL Monument is one of the last almost "unspoiled"
wildernesses—which means it is relatively unmarked by man. Yet it
is already, despite being one of the latest-explored parts of the continent, a palimpsest of human history, speculation, rumor, fantasy, ambi-
tion, science, controversy, and conflicting plans for use, and these
human records so condition our responses to the place that they contain a good part of Dinosaur's meaning.

What shall we say of it? That it is a three-pronged district of about
200,000 acres, straddling the Utah-Colorado border a little south of
where that border meets the southern boundary of Wyoming. That
it is a part—one of the junior partners—of the National Park System
begun with the reservation of Yellowstone in 1872 and confirmed by
the establishment of the National Park Service in 1916. That topographi-
cally it is defined by the deep canyons of two rivers, the Green and
the Yampa, which meet secretly in the sunny, sunken pocket of Echo
Park and then together cut Whirlpool Canyon, Island Park, Rainbow
Park, and Split Mountain Canyon, from whose mouth the water breaks
out into the open Uinta Valley of Utah. That the plateau through which
the canyons are cut is an eastward extension of the Uinta Mountains,
one of the few east-west-trending ranges in the United States. That
the larger of the two rivers, the Green, is the longest fork of the Colorado; and that it used to be called the Seedskeedee-Agie, the Prairie
Hen River, by the Crows, and by the Spaniards the Rio Verde. Its
tributary the Yampa is even yet by some people and some maps called
the Bear.

One can observe that Echo Park, at the heart of this reserve, lies
at approximately 109° West Longitude and 40°31′ North Latitude; that
the altitude ranges from 4,700 feet at the mouth of Split Mountain

Castle Park, Dinosaur National Monument

Canyon to 9,600 feet at the tip of Zenobia Peak near the northeastern boundary; that the rocks exposed run in age from the Uinta Mountain quartzite of the Pre-Cambrian period to the Brown's Park sandstone of the Pliocene; that the life zones represented spread from the Sonoran in the canyon bottoms to sub-arctic on the higher ridges. The colors of the rocks vary from a rich red-brown to vermilion, from gray to almost sugar-white, with many shades of pink and buff and salmon in between. The cliffs and sculptured forms are sometimes smooth, sometimes fantastically craggy, always massive, and they have a peculiar capacity to excite the imagination; the effect on the human spirit is neither numbing nor awesome, but warm and infinitely peaceful.

Having assembled these facts, both objective and subjective, we have said very little. Even the dry facts are simply the generalizations of human observation, distillations of topographical, cartographical, geological, biological, and other work that men have done in the region. Describing a place, we inevitably describe the marks human beings have put upon a place, the uses they have put it to, the things they have been taught by it. Even the dinosaurs whose bodies grounded on the bar of a Jurassic river here 120,000,000 years ago, and whose petrified bones gave the Monument its first reason for reservation as well as its permanent and rather misleading name, were only rocks until human curiosity unearthed and studied and compared and interpreted them.

To describe Dinosaur one must begin by summarizing its human history, and human history in Dinosaur is quaintly begun in the completely human impulse to immortalize oneself by painting or pecking or carving one's private mark, the symbol of one's incorrigible identity, on rocks and trees.

The prehistoric people who inhabited the Green and Yampa canyons, and who belonged to the cultural complex known to archaeologists as the Fremont Culture, a laggard branch of the prehistoric Pueblo-Basketmaker group, or Anasazi, left pictographs and petroglyphs which they painted in red ocher or chipped with sharp stones in the faces of the cliffs that mark the northernmost extension of the Anasazi Culture. These murals, together with the terrace camp sites and middens and the many storage granaries in caves, are among the earliest human marks in the area. To us, the most immediately fascinating of the relics the Fremont people left are these pictures, which record the game they hunted, the ceremonial objects they revered, the idle doodling dreams they indulged in, and—most wistful and most human of all—the painted handprints and footprints, the personal tracks, that said, and still say: "I am."

These are all of Dinosaur's history for a long time; they reflect the period from about A.D. 400–800. some archaeologists believe that on the Uinta and Yampa plateaus there may be evidences of the passage southward, sometime about the year 1000, of the Athapascan hunters who were the ancestors of the modern Navajo and Apache, but the origin of those camp sites is still speculative. Leaving out that possibility, there passed nearly a thousand years after the last of the Fremont people departed during which, as far as history knows, these canyons were only wind and water and stone, space and sky and the slow sandpapering of erosion, the unheard scurry of lizard and scream of mountain lion, the unseen stiff-legged caution of deer, the unnoted roar of rapids in the dark slot of Lodore and the unrecorded blaze of canyon color darkening with rain and whitening with snow and glaring in the high sun of solstice.

When the next man left a mark, he was a Spaniard, one of a watchful vanguard. The year was 1776. And nobody later reported seeing the mark he left; we know he left it only because Fray Silvestre Vélez

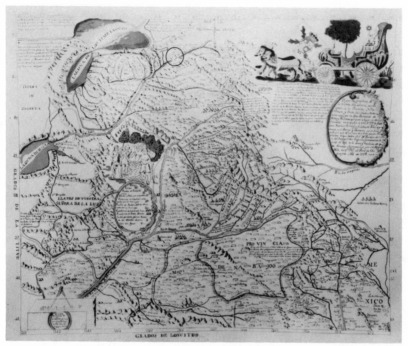

Miera's map of the Escalante Expedition. Circled near top center is the location of "Sierra Mineral"—today's Split Mountain.

de Escalante made an entry in his diary for September 14 as he was camped on the bank of the Green on his way to seek a route from New Mexico to Monterey in California.

"In this place," the explorer wrote (it was the day when the British were moving in to occupy New York, and General George Washington was preparing his retreat to Harlem Heights), "there are six large black cottonwood trees that have grown in pairs, attached to one another, and they are the ones closest to the river. Near them is another, standing alone, on whose trunk, on the side facing the northwest, Don Joaquin Lain with an adz cleared a small space in the form of a rectangular window, and with a chisel carved on it the letters and numbers of this inscription, *The Year 1776;* and lower down in different letters the name *Lain,* with two crosses outside, the larger one above the inscription and the smaller one below it."

There are still cottonwoods answering that description near the southern boundary of the monument, a half-mile or so below the dinosaur quarry and Monument Headquarters. Almost certainly they are

not the same ones, for cottonwoods are not long-lived trees; but if
they are, as some people believe, they have proved a less durable or
less inert base for immortality than the cliffs the Fremont people
scribbled on: the living wood has overgrown and obliterated any inscription. Fortunately the passage westward of those first Spaniards,
the discoverers of the Green River among much else, was also recorded
in Escalante's diary, in the Word, the most durable of all materials.
The Word thus bounds Dinosaur not only on its southern geographical
border but at the threshold of its entrance into recorded history.

These Spaniards probably did no more than poke their noses into
the canyons, though Escalante reported in his diary "two high cliffs
which, after forming a sort of corral, come so close together that one
can scarcely see the opening through which the river comes"; and Miera
set down on his map a mountain he called Sierra Mineral that was
split straight through by the river. Both journal entry and the Sierra
Mineral are surely references to Split Mountain.

Except for that tempting glimpse, Escalante skirted the southern
edge of the cut-up Uinta and Yampa uplifts. Other travelers would
skirt them along the north, leaving a no-man's-land between the known
routes called the California Trail and the Spanish Trail. The canyons
were a barrier, not a highway. But the next mark that men made in
them recorded an attempt to use the river as highway, and to link
the Spanish-dominated country southward with the routes of trappers
and mountain men just finding their way across the continental divide
among the headwaters of the Green.

That next mark came forty-nine years after Escalante. Like Lain's
inscription on the tree (and, for all we know, like the murals of the
Fremont people), it recorded a name and a date.

"Ashley, 1825," it says. It is painted on a rock in Red Canyon, above
Brown's Park and outside the present Dinosaur National Monument.
It commemorated the first known penetration of the Green River's
canyons by white men—the bullboat expedition of General William
Henry Ashley and six mountain men from about the site of present
Fontanelle, Wyoming, to somewhere in Desolation Canyon, below
the Uinta Valley. The purpose, like Escalante's, was practical: the exploration of a route, this time for profitable fur trade and a more
southerly rendezvous among the Utes. Like Escalante's, the route
turned out to have serious defects, and was not soon used again. Moreover, the written accounts of the journey waited a long time to be

made public. Nevertheless, history lost and then found again is still history.

Ashley had divided his party of mountain men into four brigades because Crows had run off many of his horses and left him overloaded. With six men and the bulk of the supplies, he pushed off from a point about fifteen miles above the mouth of the Sandy, hoping to open up the southern country to the fur trade. Into the teeth of the unknown—into the teeth, in fact, of wild and fearful rumors, such as the one promoted by his own employee and partisan James Beckwourth of an awesome "suck" "where the river enters the Utah Mountains"—Ashley ran his laden bullboats. At Henry's Fork, where he appointed a rendezvous, and in Brown's Hole, where he found that several thousand Indians had wintered, he was in known country, or semi-known. But the run through Red Canyon's rapids had given them a good shaking and had made them unload and portage all their goods and lower the bullboats over one drop on rawhide cords. That was at Ashley Falls, named later by another explorer who had no idea who Ashley was; and that was where he took five minutes to paint his name on the rock.

The rest of his trip left no marks on the country. Through Lodore, which impressed them all with its gloom and scared them with its wild water, they went as unnoted as bubbles of foam; caught their breath in the lovely bottoms of Echo Park; ran or portaged through Whirlpool and Split Mountain canyons, still, of course, unnamed. In Split Mountain, Ashley was within an eyelash of drowning; his man Beckwourth later made claims to a heroic rescue. Actually when Ashley was running the canyons Beckwourth was clear over on the other side of the mountains with James Clyman's and then with Thomas Fitzpatrick's brigade.

Ashley's journal was not found and published until 1918. His scoot down the canyons in a flimsy pole framework covered with buffalo hide and calked with pitch was a casual episode in a career notable for fortitude and daring, and it had no effect on history because history never heard of it until much other history had overtaken and passed it. As it happened, the painted name and date on the rock by Ashley Falls stood there under rain and sun another twenty-four years before white men again came that way, and when they came they barely noticed the name and had no notion who had left it there.

They came on their way to somewhere else, part of the stream pouring across the northern passes bound for the gold fields of California in 1849. Their motive in running the river was not exploration, but impatience; their resource was not the cool daring of Ashley, but foolhardiness; and they knew nothing, neither geography nor history, to help or to deter them.

They were bullwhackers on a Forty-niner wagon train, fed up with dust and the poky plod of oxen, and displeased by the train-leader's decision to winter in Salt Lake City because of the lateness of the season. They said: By golly, if only a river would show up, and if they had a boat, and if it looked as if the water might flow to the Pacific, for a two-bit shinplaster they would . . . So the river showed up, and rumor said it ran to the Pacific, and at the edge, like something provided in a fable, lay a sunken barge that had been built as a ferry. They did not bother to think. They patched up the barge and loaded their gear into it, and when the wagon train pulled out for Salt Lake City the seven bullwhackers pried themselves off the mudbank and headed downriver.

God was good to them; at least He let them live. But He kept them pretty busy. At Ashley Falls they ran their barge among the rocks and couldn't budge it. Undaunted, they made two canoes out of pine trees and lashed them together to make a kind of catamaran. When that appeared insufficient to carry their stuff, they stopped and made another.

On those cobbled craft the seven somehow got through Lodore; within it, at Disaster Falls, they found a wrecked skiff and a note on a tree saying that their unknown predecessor was getting out to Salt Lake by land. As trackless as driftwood, which they resembled, they floated through Whirlpool and Split Mountain and into the Uinta Valley, and through it, and on through Desolation and Gray canyons to about the site of modern Greenriver, Utah. Their taste for river voyaging was somewhat dampened, but their ignorance of geography—in which they were not alone in 1849—might even then have persuaded them to risk the river trail farther if the Ute chief Walkara, or Walker, had not taken pity on the misguided Mericats and talked them too into going overland to Salt Lake City, there to catch on with another wagon train. Their story was told many years later by one of their number, W. L. Manly, in a book called *Death Valley in '49*.

So except for the healed or rotted inscription in the cottonwood on its southern boundary, and the name of Ashley just outside its northern prong, Dinosaur had no recorded white history until past the middle of the nineteenth century. Escalante's discoveries had leaked into American consciousness indirectly, by way of Baron von Humboldt's 1810 map of New Spain, which was based partly on the map made by Escalante's companion Miera. But nobody had heard of Ashley or Manly, and it was reserved for the third man through the canyons to be their effective discoverer. He came with no other purpose than to know; he was in search of *this* country, not on his way somewhere else.

On May 12, 1869, the first transcontinental railroad train crossed the Green at Green River, Wyoming Territory, and the first period of Western history was over. And as they crossed, the first transcontinental tourists reclining in the palace cars exchanged waves with the last continental explorers, who were calking their boats below the bridge. Those last explorers were Major John Wesley Powell's Colorado River Exploring Expedition, and they were not only closing one phase of the West but opening another. This one-armed veteran of the Union army, preparing his ten men and four boats for a raid on the unknown canyons, was later to have a greater effect on the development of the West than any other man.

He was probably . . . not an especially good white-water man; and, more than that, he was the first, so far as he knew. Though he had all the available information, including maps, he did not have much. He ran almost as blind as Ashley had, through a country still patched with guesswork and rumor. Though he saw Ashley's inscription in Red Canyon, he had no idea who Ashley was, and he misread the date as 1855 and guessed that Ashley must have been a prospector.

Powell was not the first explorer of these canyons; but he was the first explorer who "took." He brought the arts of written record along with him, he measured and mapped as he went, he left a trail that led backward into the broad migration track of western civilization. Working his four heavy, awkward, overloaded boats laboriously down and over and around rapids and falls, he named what he passed, and behind him the canyons stretched northward to the railroad, forever now a part of human knowledge.

John Wesley Powell

He passed and misread Ashley's daub, passed Brown's Park (then called Brown's Hole) with its tracks of Indian and fur-trader and rustler and horse thief and its ruins of old Fort Davy Crockett, earlier called Fort Misery, left over from fur-trade days. Once he dropped through the Gate of Lodore, which is for practical purposes the northern river entrance to the present Monument, the map and its names are his: the Canyon of Lodore, Disaster Falls, where he lost a boat, Triplet Falls, Hell's Half Mile, Echo Park and Steamboat Rock, Whirlpool Canyon and Island Park and Split Mountain. The accounts written by himself and the men of his party for various newspapers were the first reports on that country, except for Jim Beckwourth's monumental lies, that the world at large saw. The photographs taken by his photographers E. O. Beaman and Jack Hillers in the next few years were the first pictorial record, and brought the canyons to the parlor stereoscopes of the nation. Powell's own *Report on the Exploration of the Colorado River of the West* remains one of the great Western adventure stories, as well as a cornerstone of early geology.

The Major hung on to this country which he had opened. He ran the canyons again in 1871, and he was exploring the area by land all through the seventies. He clarified the whole region of the Plateau Province, stretching all the way from Wyoming to modern Lake Mead, and in person or through his collaborators he gave it not merely a map and names, but much of its geological history and an explanation of its forms. Reading the rocks of this country so strange, so unstudied, and so perfectly exposed by the cutting edges of the rivers, he produced a second monograph, *The Geology of the Uinta Mountains of Utah and a Portion of Country Adjacent Thereto,* and in that book and its predecessor, the *Exploration,* laid the foundations for much of the modern science of geomorphology. In the area east and south of Dinosaur, among the White River and Uinta Utes, he began studies of the native tribes that eventually made him, in the words of Spencer Baird of the Smithsonian, the one who "knew more about the live Indian than any live man."

The real discoverer of the Dinosaur canyons was the man who brought knowledge to them, and that man was Powell. Though Clarence King's Survey of the 40th Parallel worked across the northern edge of the Uintas in the late sixties, and both F. V. Hayden and the celebrated paleontologist Othniel C. Marsh had touched the fringes a year or two later, it was Powell who penetrated the country and made it his own. King, Hayden, and Marsh all persist on the map as names of high Uinta peaks, but Powell's mark is all over the map. He is the *genius loci* of Dinosaur, as of all the canyons of the Green and Colorado. Schoolmaster to the nation, explorer, enthusiast, planner, and prophet, he probably affected more lives in the West than any of our Presidents have, and it was from the canyons of Dinosaur that he drew much of his early knowledge and the hints that a long career would develop into policies of land and water and settlement vital to half the continent.

But it was not Major Powell who got the Dinosaur canyons preserved as part of the National Park System, and not he who gave the Monument its somewhat misleading name. That, or the beginning of it, was the work of another enthusiast, less illustrious but quite as dedicated, named Earl Douglass.

Douglass, like Powell, was a frontier farm boy, self-made, partly self-educated. When he came into the Uinta Valley he was already a distinguished field geologist, paleontologist, and botanist. . . . He first conducted a search through the Uinta Valley because a hunch told him that giant bones reported by sheepherders meant a real deposit, a regular dinosaur quarry, somewhere near. And he was encouraged in his bone-hunting by Andrew Carnegie, who sent him out on a personal commission to find things to fill the Carnegie Museum's Hall of Vertebrate Paleontology in Pittsburgh, and win people to education with something as big as a barn.

Douglass found his dinosaur deposit in August 1909, when he stumbled across a row of Brontosaur vertebrae weathered out in relief in an exposed wall of the Morrison formation below the mouth of Split Mountain Canyon. He worked the quarry under the most primitive conditions for fifteen years, scraping and blasting and chiseling at the rock, removing and labeling the bones, packing them in homemade plaster of paris cooked out of the local gypsum ledges, hauling them to the railroad dozens of miles away and shipping them back to the Carnegie Institute—700,000 pounds of them altogether.

He filled not only Carnegie's hall but many another; in almost any good paleontological museum the world around you are likely to encounter the bones of dinosaurs, big or little, carnivorous or herbivorous, that were grounded on the Jurassic bar where Monument Headquarters now stands, and were patiently picked out of the rock 120,000,000 years later by Earl Douglass and his helpers.

In a very real way, Douglass gave his life to that dinosaur grave-yard. He put his best years into it. His unfinished stone house, part of the dream he had of an irrigated homestead on the banks of the Green, still stands there with the wind lonesome through its window and door holes and the lizards alert on its sills—as eloquent an archaeo-logical monument as any the Fremont people left. Within a little fence, under homemade headstones below the dune-like Jurassic foothills of the Uintas, lie the bodies of his father and sister. These things give him a dry and whispering vested interest in the place; his innocent, laborious, enthusiastic spirit persists there.

He is also the reason why the Dinosaur Monument exists, for he found it so hard to protect his diggings from souvenir-hunters that he had to do something. At first he tried to take out a mineral claim, but found that bones, even petrified ones, were not among the minerals. So he appealed to the Carnegie Museum, and the Museum took its influence to Washington, and on October 4, 1915, Woodrow Wilson by proclamation set aside the eighty acres around the quarry as Dino-saur National Monument.

The quarry is still part of the Monument, whose headquarters build-ing sits next door. . . . But the dinosaur quarry which gave the Monu-ment its name is no more than the front-yard of the people's park here established. Back of this natural schoolroom . . . is the living laboratory of the Green and Yampa canyons stretching all the way from the mouth of Split Mountain to Steamboat Rock, and from that natural dividing cliff up the Yampa to Lily Park and up the Green through Lodore to Brown's Park.

The canyons were added to the Dinosaur National Monument by proclamation of Franklin D. Roosevelt on July 14, 1938, in a move which was part of the national rescue operation to save eroded range lands and mined Dust Bowl fields and endangered watersheds and half-spoiled wilderness areas from total ruin. The consciousness of national guilt and mismanagement, and the press of necessity, were strong then; they are less strong now, when partially successful rescue work and a rainier cycle have temporarily healed some of the scars of the thir-ties. To this moment, at least, the Green and Yampa canyons have been saved intact, a wilderness that is the property of all Americans, a 325-square-mile preserve that is part schoolroom and part playground and part—the best part—sanctuary from a world paved with concrete, jet-propelled, smog-blanketed, sterilized, over-insured, aseptic; a world

Gates of Lodore

mass-produced with interchangeable parts, and with every natural beautiful thing endangered by the raw engineering power of the twentieth century.

We live in the Antibiotic Age, and Antibiotic means literally "against life." We had better not be against life. That is the way to become as extinct as the dinosaurs. And if, as the population experts were guessing in November 1954, the human race will (other things being equal) have increased so much in the next three hundred years that we will have only a square yard of ground apiece to stand on, then we may want to take turns running to some preserved place such as Dinosaur. *How much wilderness do the wilderness-lovers want?* ask those who would mine and dig and cut and dam in such sanctuary spots as these. The answer is easy: *Enough so that there will be in the years ahead a little relief, a little quiet, a little relaxation, for any of our increasing millions who need and want it.* That means we need as much wilderness as can still be saved. There isn't much left, and there is no more where the old open spaces came from.

Perhaps, when the Jurassic equivalent of a hornet stung a dinosaur somewhere out along his eighty or ninety feet of tail, it may have taken him ten or fifteen minutes to get the word. Even when he had a regional organization, the so-called "second brain" of the Stegosaurus, he was mentally retarded; his reactions were slow, with results that we can read in the rocks of the quarry in Dinosaur National Monument.

It should not take us so long as it took Stegosaurus to get word that is vital to us. There is some evidence already that we run the risk of an over-specialization as fatal as that of the sauropods—we may over-engineer ourselves. The vital wilderness, the essential hoarded living-space, the open and the green and the quiet, might not survive the bulldozer as readily as they survived Ashley's bullboats and Manly's bullwhackers.

A place is nothing in itself. It has no meaning, it can hardly be said to exist, except in terms of human perception, use, and response. The wealth and resources and usefulness of any region are only inert potential until man's hands and brain have gone to work; and natural beauty is nothing until it comes to the eye of the beholder. The natural world, actually, is the test by which each man proves himself: I see, I feel, I love, I use, I alter, I appropriate, therefore I am. Or the natural world is a screen onto which we project our own images; without our images there, it is as blank as the cold screen of an empty movie house. We cannot even describe a place except in terms of its human uses.

And as the essential history of Dinosaur is its human history, the only possible destruction of Dinosaur will be a human destruction. Admittedly it would be idiotic to preach conservation of such a wilderness in perpetuity, just to keep it safe from all human use. It is only for human use that it has any meaning, or is worth preserving. But there is a vast difference among uses. Some uses use things *up* and some last forever. Recreation, properly controlled, is a perpetual use, and a vital one. It is possible to make such a wilderness as Dinosaur accessible without ruining it, and more than possible that its value for human relief from twentieth-century strains and smells and noises will prove greater than its problematic, limited, and short-term value for water or power, especially when those values can be had at other sites without violating this unique and beautiful canyon sanctuary.

We have learned something of what we risk when we mess around with nature's balances. If we destroy even so apparently worthless and harmful an item as down timber in a forest, we destroy the home of insects and grubs that are the food of certain birds. Destroying their food, we drive the birds out or thin them out, and in so doing we remove one of the principal policing agents. Deprived of its winged police, our nice cleaned-up forest may be infected with sudden devastating pests, more virulent and less controllable than anything that nature's checks and balances have permitted before.

Eventually we may learn that it is quite dangerous to remake without sufficient precaution the total face of the planet, to turn our bulldozers and earth-movers loose just because we *can*.

Back in the canyons of the Green and Yampa, and in the pockets along side streams, there have been hermits and squatters and isolated ranchers from the 1870's on. One of them, old Pat Lynch, heard about Echo Park from his friend Major Powell and settled there probably in the seventies. During many years in the canyons he spread himself; he was a one-man Occupation of what was called locally Pat's Hole. He had cabins and cave shelters in both Echo Park and Castle Park; a cave on the Rial Chew ranch on Pool Creek still contains some of his personal belongings and his sapling bed. Castle Park seems to have been the real Pat's Hole, headquarters of Pat's occupation, for in the possession of Charley Mantle is a notice which says: "To all who this may consarn that I Pat Lynch do lay claim on this botom for my home and support Wrote the 8th month of 1886 by P L ynch."

Pat was the first white man to use the Yampa and Green river canyons, and he used them both for his livelihood and for his pleasure. He did not neglect immortality: his private petroglyph, a ship under full sail, is pecked into a cliff in Castle Park to link his spirit with Fremont man and Ute and Spaniard and fur-trade partisan. He was a cultural horizon: University of Colorado archaeologists excavating Hell's Midden found a whole clearly defined layer, already covered with silt and dirt, containing the suspender buttons, cartridge cases, and other artifacts and relics of Pat Lynch's authentic life.

But the most characteristic of the remains he left is one that might be used as a motto by all the increasing users of the canyons who have come after him. In a cave that had been one of Pat's shelters, the Mantles found a note. It said, in the brogue that cropped out even in Pat's writing:

> *If in those caverns you shelter take*
> *Plais do to them no harm*
> *Lave everything you find around hanging up or on the*
> *ground.*

That is all conservation is about. That is all the National Parks are about. Use, but do no harm.

It is legitimate to hope that there may [be] left in Dinosaur the special kind of human mark, the special record of human passage, that distinguishes man from all other species. It is rare enough among men, impossible to any other form of life. *It is simply the deliberate and chosen refusal to make any marks at all.* Sometimes we have withheld our power to destroy, and have left a threatened species like the buffalo, a threatened beauty spot like Yosemite or Yellowstone or Dinosaur, scrupulously alone. We are the most dangerous species of life on the planet, and every other species, even the earth itself, has cause to fear our power to exterminate. But we are also the only species which, when it chooses to do so, will go to great effort to save what it might destroy.

It is a better world with some buffalo left in it, a richer world with some gorgeous canyons unmarred by signboards, hot-dog stands, super highways, or high-tension lines, undrowned by power or irrigation reservoirs. If we preserved as parks only those places that have no economic possibilities, we would have no parks. And in the decades to come, it will not be only the buffalo and the trumpeter swan who need sanctuaries. Our own species is going to need them too.

It needs them now.

Bernard De Voto

EPILOGUE:
FOOTLOOSE IN DEMOCRACY

*D*e Voto came late to the parks, late to conservationism. *Although a native of Utah, and long identified as an authority on the West by his readers, he did not travel extensively in the region until the summer of 1946, when he was forty-nine. Most of his professional life was spent in the East, as a journalist, historian, critic, editor, teacher, and novelist. In everything he was a controversialist. "Genius is Not Enough," his estimation of Thomas Wolfe, is one of the high points of invective in American letters. His lively assessments of Mark Twain's life and work brought him a wide, if not always respectful, audience. Since 1935 he had conducted his opinions to the public from "The Easy Chair,"* Harper's Magazine's *venerable column of comment. And just before he left on his 1946 trip, he finished his masterful rendition of westward expansion,* Across the Wide Missouri; *it won a Pulitzer Prize the next year.*

What De Voto saw in the West changed him for good. Not only did he gain, in the words of his biographer Wallace Stegner, "the geographical expertise that most of his readers assumed he already possessed," he awakened to conservationism and acquainted himself first-hand with the national parks. He later confided to a friend that the trip was "by far the best thing I ever did in my life."

From then on until his death in 1955, he was committed. Whenever a warning was needed, De Voto shouted. He spearheaded a successful counterattack against ranchers who wanted to maneuver public-domain grazing rights into their own pockets. He defended the U.S. Forest Service against those who would emasculate it. And, as we have seen, he weighed in early against the Echo Park dam plans.

To his credit, De Voto was not one to be swept away by the glamour of the national parks; he was willing to get behind the scenes and address issues which the public rarely notices, such as Park Service morale. In one of his more audacious Easy Chairs, he first excoriated the government for the outrageous rents it charged rangers for dilapidated quarters, and then called for closing the largest national parks until Congress voted enough money for the Park Service to properly maintain them in the face of the post-war crush of visitors.

In nine years he wrote nearly forty combative articles on conservation. Almost all of them were published in general-interest magazines with large readerships from which more converts could be drawn. In this final selection, which appeared in Fortune *magazine in 1947, De Voto appraises the parks from his vantage point as an unrepentant "small-d democrat."*

FOR A nation that grows more metropolitan and industrialized every year the experience of solitude, even the simple fact of quiet, has become inestimable. It is the more exigent in that the memory of the American people keeps alive a need for the wilderness that shaped us, that was our birthright, and that we have despoiled. It is imperative to maintain portions of the wilderness untouched, so that a tree will rot where it falls, a waterfall will pour its curve without generating electricity, a trumpeter swan may float on uncontaminated water—and moderns may at least see what their ancestors knew in their nerves and blood.

At the more generally visited parks a small percentage of visitors use the "package tours" sold by railroad companies and travel agencies. For a fixed price the tourist buys a fixed tour; his accommodations are reserved for him, his baggage is taken care of, competent guides conduct him to all the celebrated sights. The fixed tour, however, is the least satisfactory way of visiting a park: it makes private wandering or individual discovery impossible, it may be exhausting, it tends to become trite. The automobile tourist does better, since he may go where he chooses and stay anywhere as long as he likes. Accommodations for him within the parks are adjusted to a caste system. At the bourgeois level there are cabin camps, usually called lodges or chalets and usually more satisfying than the hotels. Finally, there are public campgrounds, where the tourist pitches his own tent or else rents one from the concessionaire and sets up housekeeping on his own.

There is a point where touring ceases to be sightseeing, one of the most fatiguing of human activities, and becomes a more profound educational or emotional or aesthetic experience. Few visitors to the parks reach that point; they do not stay long enough. The deeper evocations of spectacle and beauty require time and tranquillity of mind; they do not come at a glance. Moreover, all the large parks and most of the others have high country or back country—usually the same—which is hard to reach and cannot be seen by anyone in a hurry. Thus it happens that two classes of people get more from the parks than anyone else.

The first class is the habitués and fanatics who return to the same park every year, sometimes from childhood to old age. They are connoisseurs, virtuosos, scholars, pedants; they resent as interlopers the swarm of tourists who lack their erudition and they condescend to the Park Service. They are all lovers and some of them are mystics: their private park has become part of their identity. More practically, they are invaluable to the Park Service for they are the minutemen who as individuals or organizations spring to arms whenever it is under attack. Their private love is a public virtue.

The other class is sometimes called, even by an occasional park ranger, the proletariat. There can be no doubt that those who stay in the public campgrounds come to learn more of the parks and get more from them than any other tourists. The campgrounds are the finest achievement of the parks, the most admirable of their public services. They have grown steadily more popular, which means that they have grown more congested, straining the ability of the park personnel to maintain them without harm to the surroundings. The gregariousness of tourists crowds the more popular camps to the limit, so that the struggle to keep them sanitary and unlittered is onerous, while other camps perhaps more pleasing will be all but empty. Thus in the valley of Yosemite, tents will be packed so thick that their occupants have to hedge them round with blankets for a minimum of privacy, while the splendid camps at the Tuolumne Meadows and elsewhere in the high country may be unoccupied.

In such camps (always picturesquely sited), in trailers and every known kind of tent, with outfits that range from the barest necessities to a truckload of household furnishings, tourists settle down for long stays. They get supplies at the general stores and to some extent can live off the land, for many of the parks are notable fishing grounds. They become friends overnight and are citizens of a community at once local and transcontinental. They are any American crowd, which means that they are equalitarian, good-natured, and destructive. (No park sign is safe when the firewood runs out, flowers will be picked under the notice that forbids their being touched, souvenirs will be chipped off or names carved on any landmark unless a ranger is at hand.) But their destructiveness is a compound of ignorance and innocence. They respond to instruction and have an eager thirst for it.

In its original mandate from the Forty-second Congress seventy-five years ago, setting aside Yellowstone as the first national park, the park administration was officially charged with solving an insoluble dilemma. It was directed to preserve the indicated areas from "injury or spoliation" and to retain them in their "natural conditions"—and also to maintain each of them as a "public park or pleasuring ground of the people." But the moment wilderness is used at all it ceases in some degree to be wilderness. To construct a road or a trail will increase the benefit and enjoyment of the people but it may also disturb the balance of nature, changing the botanical or perhaps even the geological conditions of the area. The problem of the service is thus to accommodate the parks to increasing numbers of visitors while preventing impairment or deterioration.

The problem is peculiarly difficult since almost all who visit the parks must do so as tourists on vacation, and therefore they desire, besides scenery, some of the holiday release that the American vacation implies. Government regulation stops at the park boundaries; beyond them the amusement business is free to construct Coney Islands and summer-resort slums unchecked. The freedom of these border operators saddens the firmly regulated concessionaires inside the parks, who provide food and lodgings at prices approved by the park superintendent. Since dilemmas are the routine business of the service, it is able to keep this one in hand; but a minority of its officials deprecate worldly pleasures and would prefer to develop the parks as sanctuaries or spiritual retreats.

Called "purists" by colleagues who disagree with them, they speak of the parks as places of re-creation, not recreation, and are a little doleful because visitors desire activities other than the superb educational ones the service provides. They veer toward the uplift, forgetting that the vulgar and even the damned are co-proprietors of the parks. They necessarily lose out. Beauty and inspiration are quite as satiating as the pleasures of the earth-bound; and a tourist may carry the ineffable unimpaired from Bright Angel to a cocktail bar. The problem is not to discourage amiable diversions but to scotch every effort, however slight, to convert the parks into summer resorts.

Since the people using the parks have leisure and free will, they get in full measure what the parks have to offer. Well, what do they get? What justifies the national parks?

First of all, silence. In any park three minutes' walk will permit you to be alone in the primeval, and this single fact is enough to justify the entire national-park system. Moreover you will enjoy the intimacy of nature as your forefathers knew it. The parks are not the only places in the U.S. where the order of nature is undisturbed, but they are the only places where the public at large can ever get at it. Our civilization excludes steadily increasing numbers of Americans from first-hand knowledge of nature—streams, plants, forests, animals, birds, even the effects of storms—and yet their need of it can never be extinguished. The parks are at once preserves, exhibits, and theatres of nature going on. The proof of their value is the wonder of tourists at so simple a thing as a beaver dam, their eagerness for instruction in anything from ecology to volcanology or from glaciers to the habits of jays, and the speed with which their naiveté becomes intelligent inquiry.

The national parks preserve not only the organic relationship of nature, they also preserve the extremes of natural spectacle and natural beauty. Both the extremity and the fact that it is preserved inviolate must be stressed. One need but think of a palisade so erected in Yosemite that the falls could be seen only after the payment of admission at a turnstile, of a pitchman selling specimens chipped from Sun Temple in Mesa Verde, or of a Ferris wheel turning where Bright Angel Trail begins. The fulfillment that beauty and spectacle have for the human spirit is not easily phrased—it relates to the depths of consciousness and to the unconscious. If the simple experience of uncontaminated nature is inestimably good, so is such an equally simple experience as glimpsing the processes of creation in what the Colorado River and the wind and rain have done at the Grand Canyon—or how a glacier has gutted a peak, how a mountain range has slipped and folded along a fault line, how in the aeons of time the fundamental earth has been erected and then redistributed grain by grain.

No one can say fully what sublimity means, or how the awe or terror or exaltation inspired by the earth in torment affects him; but everyone, even the shallowest sightseer, the strident and aggressive woman in purple rayon slacks shouldering others aside to look at the Great White Throne, is enlarged by the experience. The sightseer may lack vocabulary, even concept, to speak of the one in the many, eternity moving through forms of change, the flowing away at once of time and earth, but there remain mystery and the fulfillment of identity, and he will be richer than he was. It is the same with aesthetics: one may lack words to express the impact of beauty but no one who has felt it remains untouched. It is renewal, enlargement, intensification. The parks preserve it permanently in the inheritance of the American citizen.

Glosses

JOHN MUIR: A MEETING IN THE VALLEY

Mrs Prof E Carr: Jeanne Carr, a friend of Muir's whose advice and encouragement helped shape his intellect as a young man

Mr Hutchings mill: a sawmill owned by James Hutchings, the other leading denizen of the Valley and Muir's employer

Mts Dana and Gabb: Dana and *Gibbs* are adjacent Sierra Nevada peaks on Yosemite's eastern boundary; possibly a misspelling by Muir

Tuolumne meadows: in the eastern part of the park

Bloody Cañon: just east of the park

Mariposa big trees: sequoia grove on the southern boundary of the park

Clark's Station: tourist camp established by Galen Clark; the site is now known as Wawona

Samoset: Pemaquid sagamore, noted for greeting the Pilgrims (in English) upon their arrival in the New World

Wachusett and Monadnock: peaks in Massachusetts and New Hampshire, respectively

OWEN WISTER: OLD YELLOWSTONE DAYS

George: not further identified

discipline and law at the sergeant's cabin: from 1886 until 1916 the park was patrolled by troops from the U.S. Army

James Bridger: fur trader and frontiersman

the Thumb: the western arm of Yellowstone Lake

Lowell: textile mill town in Massachusetts, famous as the first American city to be planned around Industrial Revolution technology (and, since 1978, the site of Lowell National Historical Park)

the Cañon: the Grand Canyon of the Yellowstone River

Norris: a junction in the park and site of a geyser basin

Lake: Yellowstone Lake

MARY ROBERTS RINEHART: RIDE THE ROCKIES AND SAVE YOUR SOUL

Howard Eaton: one of the originators of dude ranching in the West

Bad Lands: of North Dakota, along the Little Missouri River, some of which are now in Theodore Roosevelt National Park

RUDYARD KIPLING: ON TOUR THROUGH THE YELLOWSTONE
Rayment: a tour operator
T. Cook and Son: Thomas Cook and Son, the foremost British travel agency
those pink and white terraces not long ago destroyed by earthquake in New Zealand: possibly a reference to an earthquake of September 1888 which struck north of Christchurch
Myanoshita: a hot-springs near Yokohama, visited earlier by Kipling on his journey
Cook City: Cooke City, Montana, the northeastern entrance to the park
tiffin: a midday meal
Cable, "Uncle Remus" Harris: George Washington Cable and Joel Chandler Harris, Southern regionalist writers
"California" howled: a reference to an incident earlier in *From Sea to Sea* in which Kipling and a temporary companion nicknamed "California" successfully fished for salmon in Oregon

JOHN BURROUGHS: DIVINE ABYSS
Charles Dudley Warner: American editor and novelist; he collaborated with Mark Twain on *The Gilded Age* (1873)
Lyell's doctrine of uniformitarianism: a doctrine of the British geologist Sir Charles Lyell, stating that geological change is more or less incremental, rather than catastrophic

CARL SANDBURG: SCRAPERS OF THE DEEP WINDS
Powell: John Wesley Powell, explorer of the Canyon
Hance: John Hance, early homesteader and tourist guide on the South Rim and teller of tall tales
Fred Harvey; El Tovar: the concession company on the South Rim; its largest hotel

THOMAS WOLFE: GULPING THE GREAT WEST
Bent: misspelling of the town of Bend, Oregon
C: Ray Conway
------: Wolfe's omission; probably the town of Merced, California
Kingman, Needles: desert towns in Arizona and California, respectively, on the main road from southern California to Grand Canyon
the National Forest beginning: Kaibab National Forest
Williams: a town at the junction of a spur road to Grand Canyon
Big Gorgooby: In the first instance, Wolfe's name for the Grand Canyon itself; later he uses it to refer to the Colorado River

rudeeleven: an uncertain word

Fred Harvey: the tourist concessioner on the South Rim

G: Gorgooby, the Grand Canyon

unvital: another uncertain word

Alberdene: not further identified

Small Gorgooby gorge: the canyon of the Little Colorado River, which inter-
sects the Grand Canyon

Cameron: town on the Little Colorado just east of the park

Browns: not further identified

Hiawatha chanting the U. P.: the Union Pacific Railroad Company, tourist
concessioner on the North Rim; also, perhaps, a pun on the abbreviation
for Michigan's Upper Peninsula, part of the setting for Longfellow's poem

M: Edward M. Miller

the great one spaced with even windows: a long tunnel on the road into
Zion Canyon

H.: not further identified

FREDERICK LAW OLMSTED: PRESERVATION FOR ALL

alone prevented the establishment of a saw mill within it: this injunction
was soon ignored, for shortly thereafter James Hutchings established a sawmill in the Valley at which John Muir worked when he first came to
Yosemite in 1869

the giant tree before referred to: the Grizzly Giant in the Mariposa Grove

JAMES BRYCE: SHOULD CARS BE ALLOWED IN YOSEMITE?

wheels of the vehicles: i.e., of horse-drawn carriages

it is also agreeably seen in riding or driving: riding horses or driving in
carriages, not cars

Mount Desert Island: off the coast of Maine, and centerpiece of Acadia
National Park

CHARLES DICKENS: THE FACTORIES OF LOWELL

Newgate: a London prison

on this side of the Atlantic: i.e., Europe

those great haunts of desperate misery: English factory towns

BAYARD TAYLOR: A SECOND WORLD

Mat, Stephen: the cave guides

Mr. Miller: not further identified

MARK TWAIN: THE HAWAII VOLCANOES

Kau: district adjacent to Kilauea

Volcano House: the name of the hotel

 "North" and "South" lakes: lakes of fiery lava within the crater

WALLACE STEGNER: THE MARKS OF HUMAN PASSAGE

the dark slot of Lodore: a narrow rapids, also called the Gates of Lodore,
    on the Green River

Miera: Don Bernardo de Miera y Pacheco, cartographer to Escalante

Red Canyon, Brown's Park: canyons of the Green on the northeast edge
    of the Uinta Mountains

James Beckwourth: a mountaineer

awesome "suck": a cataract

Henry's Fork: tributary of the Green north of the Uintas

James Clyman, Thomas Fitzpatrick: mountain men and expeditioners

Greenriver, Utah: a town (also spelled Green River, as is the town in Wyo-
    ming, mentioned below)

Spencer Baird: a prominent 19th-century naturalist

Clarence King, F. V. Hayden: two of the foremost scientific explorers of
    the West

Lily Park: a rapids on the Yampa

Charley Mantle; Mantles: early settlers in the Castle Park district of Dinosaur

BERNARD DE VOTO: FOOTLOOSE IN DEMOCRACY

Bright Angel: the main trail leading down from the South Rim of the Grand
    Canyon

Great White Throne: one of the most prominent topographic features of
    Zion National Park

Sources

John Muir, *The Letters of Ralph Waldo Emerson*, edited by Ralph L. Rusk, six volumes (New York and London: Columbia University Press, 1939), 6:148–157, 201–204. *Our National Parks* (Boston and New York: Houghton Mifflin, 1901, enlarged edition 1909), 131–136.

Ralph Waldo Emerson, "Concord Hymn," in *The Chief American Poets*, edited by Curtis Hidden Page (Boston: Houghton Mifflin, 1905), 63.

Henry James, *The American Scene* (London: Chapman and Hall, 1907), 273–275, 277–279, 288–293.

Owen Wister, "Old Yellowstone Days," *Harper's* (Vol. 172, March 1936), 471–480.

Abraham Lincoln, address given at Gettysburg, Pennsylvania, 19 November 1863, reprinted in Carl Sandburg, *Abraham Lincoln: The War Years*, two volumes (New York: Harcourt, Brace & Company, 1939), 2: 469.

Mary Roberts Rinehart, "Through Glacier National Park with Howard Eaton," *Collier's* 57:6 (April 22, 1916), 11–13, 34–36; and 57:7 (April 29, 1916), 20–21, 26–28.

Rudyard Kipling, *From Sea to Sea: Letters of Travel*, two volumes (New York: Doubleday and McClure, 1899), 2:67–72, 73–80, 84–86, 96–103.

John Burroughs, "The Grand Cañon of the Colorado," *Century* 59:3 (January 1911), 425–438.

Harriet Monroe, "The Cataracts." Reprinted in Daniel J. Cahill, *Harriet Monroe* (New York: Twayne, 1973), 120–121. "Hetch-Hetchy," *Century* (Vol. 79, January 1910), 441.

Carl Sandburg, "Many Hats," in *Complete Poems* (New York: Harcourt, Brace & World, 1950), 429–435. Originally published in *Good Morning, America* (1928). Remarks on the Gettysburg Address are from *Abraham Lincoln: The War Years*, two volumes (New York: Harcourt, Brace & Company, 1939), 2:476–477.

Thomas Wolfe, *A Western Journal: A Daily Log of the Great Parks Trip* (Pittsburgh: University of Pittsburgh Press, 1951).

George Catlin, *Illustrations of the Manners, Customs, and Condition of the North American Indians, With Letters and Notes Written During Eight Years of*

Travel and Adventure Among the Wildest and Most Remarkable Tribes Now Existing, two volumes (London: Henry G. Bohn, 1866), 1:260–264.

Frederick Law Olmsted, "The Yosemite Valley and the Mariposa Big Tree Grove" (1865), reprinted as "The Yosemite Valley and the Mariposa Big Trees," edited by Laura Wood Roper, *Landscape Architecture* 43:1 (October 1952), 14–23.

James Bryce, "National Parks—The Need of the Future," in *University and Historical Addresses* (New York: Macmillan, 1913), 393–394, 397–401.

Charles Dickens, *American Notes for General Circulation* (Paris: Stassin and Xavier, 1842), 78–84.

Bayard Taylor, "The Mammoth Cave," in *Wonders of Nature as Seen and Described by Famous Writers*, edited by Esther Singleton (New York: P. F. Collier & Son, 1911), 283–294; originally published in *At Home and Abroad: A Sketch-Book of Life, Scenery and Men* (New York: G. P. Putnam, 1859); Singleton used an edition of 1864.

Mark Twain, *Roughing It* (Berkeley: University of California Press, 1972), 472–479, 484–486.

Wallace Stegner, "The Marks of Human Passage," in *This is Dinosaur: Echo Park Country and its Magic Rivers*, edited by Wallace Stegner (New York: Alfred A. Knopf, 1955), 3–17.

Bernard De Voto, "The National Parks," *Fortune* 35:6 (June 1947), 120–121.

ILLUSTRATIONS

39   Beehive Geyser by Thomas Moran, from *Scribner's Monthly*, June, 1871
42   Mary Roberts Rinehart portrait courtesy of Frederick R. Rinehart
47   Lone rider courtesy of Glacier National Park
53   Gardiner Depot courtesy of Yellowstone National Park
55   Mammoth Hot Springs Hotel courtesy of Yellowstone National Park
57   Kipling portrait from *Plain Tales of the Hills* (New York: Charles Scribner's Sons, 1899)
61   Tourists in hot springs courtesy of Yellowstone National Park
68   Grand Canyon of the Yellowstone from *Marvels of the New West*
73   Grand Canyon scene from *The Exploration of the Colorado River and its Canyons* by John Wesley Powell (New York: Dover Publications, 1961)
81   Yosemite Falls from *Marvels of the New West*
88   Grand Canyon scene from *Over the Range to the Golden Gate* by Stanley Wood (Chicago: R. R. Donnelley & Sons, Publishers, 1889)
95   Mt. Shasta scene from *Over the Range*
101   Wolfe journey map reprinted from *A Western Journal: A Daily Log of the Great Parks Trip, June 20–July 2, 1938* by Thomas Wolfe, by permission of the University of Pittsburgh Press. ©1967 by Paul Gitlin, Administrator, C.T.A.
105   Hawaii volcano scene from *Narrative of a Tour Through Hawaii, or Owhyee* by William Ellis (London: H. Fisher, 1828)
109   Bison from *Buffalo Land* by William E. Webb (Philadelphia: Hubbard Brothers, 1873)
114   Nevada Fall from *Discovery of the Yosemite*
119   Yosemite scene from *Discovery of the Yosemite*
125   Sentinel Rock from *Discovery of the Yosemite*
133   Lowell scene courtesy of the Lowell Historical Society
138   "Fat Man's Misery" from *One Hundred Miles in Mammoth Cave in 1880* by H. C. Hovey (Golden, Colorado: Outbooks, 1982)
141   Mammoth Cave scenes from *One Hundred Miles in Mammoth Cave in 1880*
148   Hawaii map from *Narrative of a Tour Through Hawaii*
151   Tourists on horseback from *One Summer in Hawaii* by Helen Mather (New York: Cassell Publishing Company, 1891)
157   Castle Park scene courtesy of Dinosaur National Monument
159   Miera map courtesy Utah State Historical Society
164   Powell portrait courtesy of Dinosaur National Monument
168   Lodore scene from *Crest of the Continent* by Ernest Ingersoll (Chicago: R. R. Donnelley & Sons, 1885)
176   Mountaintop scene courtesy of Kent and Donna Dannen

Text type   Garamond, set by Lyn Chaffee, Archetype, Denver

Display type (chapter heads)   Centaur and Arrighi, set by
Mackenzie-Harris Corp., San Francisco

Display type (cover, title page spread)   rendered by Carole
Thickstun and Lawrence Ormsby at Cave Creek, Arizona

Typography and binding design   Frederick R. Rinehart, Carole
Thickstun, and Lawrence Ormsby

SPECIAL NOTE

A 2′ × 3′ poster of the Ormsby and Thickstun title page spread to
Mirror of America may be made available by the publisher on a limited
basis. Please inquire at Post Office Box 3161, Boulder, Colorado 80303